Also by Jean Anderson

THE ART OF AMERICAN INDIAN COOKING
(with Yeffe Kimball)

THE FAMILY CIRCLE COOKBOOK
(with the Food Editors of *Family Circle*)

THE DOUBLEDAY COOKBOOK*
(with Elaine Hanna)

RECIPES FROM AMERICA'S RESTORED
VILLAGES

THE GREEN THUMB PRESERVING GUIDE

THE GRASS ROOTS COOKBOOK

JEAN ANDERSON'S PROCESSOR COOKING

HALF A CAN OF TOMATO PASTE & OTHER
CULINARY DILEMMAS** (with Ruth Buchan)

UNFORBIDDEN SWEETS

JEAN ANDERSON COOKS

THE NEW DOUBLEDAY COOKBOOK
(with Elaine Hanna)

THE FOOD OF PORTUGAL***

MICRO WAYS: EVERY COOK'S GUIDE TO
SUCCESSFUL MICROWAVING
(with Elaine Hanna)

* *Winner of two R. T. French Tastemaker Awards (1975):*
Best Basic Cookbook of the Year
and
Best Cookbook of the Year, overall

** *Winner of the R. T. French Tastemaker Award,*
Best Specialty Cookbook of the Year (1980)

*** *Winner of the Seagram/International Association of*
Cooking Professionals
Award, Best Foreign Cookbook of the Year (1986)

Jean Anderson's Sin-Free Desserts

JEAN ANDERSON'S SIN-FREE DESSERTS

150 Low-Cholesterol Desserts

Foreword by Allen W. Mead, M.D.
Preface by Barbara B. Deskins, Ph.D., R.D.

Photographs by Dennis Galante
Food Styling by Dora Jonassen

DOUBLEDAY
New York London Toronto Sydney Auckland

PUBLISHED BY DOUBLEDAY
a division of Bantam Doubleday Dell Publishing Group, Inc.
666 Fifth Avenue, New York, New York 10103

DOUBLEDAY and the portrayal of an anchor with a dolphin
are registered trademarks of Doubleday,
a division of Bantam Doubleday Dell Publishing Group, Inc.

Portions of this book have appeared in slightly different
form in *Cook's Magazine* and *Food & Wine.*

The recipe for Cloud-High Angel Food Cake first appeared
under the title "The Very Best Angel Food Cake" in *Cook's
Simple and Seasoned Cuisine* Copyright © 1988 by *Cook's Magazine.*
Reprinted by permission of Simon & Schuster, Inc.

Library of Congress Cataloging-in-Publication Data
Anderson, Jean,
[Sin free desserts]
Jean Anderson's sin free desserts : 150 low-cholesterol desserts by Jean Anderson ; with a foreword by Allen W. Mead
and a preface by Barbara B. Deskins. — 1st ed.
p.   cm.
Includes index.
1. Low-cholesterol diet—Recipes. 2. Desserts. I. Title.
RM237.75.A53   1991
641.8'6—dc20   91-9855
                                                                              CIP

BOOK DESIGN BY CAROL MALCOLM-RUSSO

ISBN 0-385-26694-4
COPYRIGHT © 1991 BY JEAN ANDERSON

ALL RIGHTS RESERVED
PRINTED IN THE UNITED STATES OF AMERICA
NOVEMBER 1991
1 3 5 7 9 10 8 6 4 2
FIRST EDITION

ACKNOWLEDGMENTS

First and foremost, I want to thank Sandra Rose Gluck, one of the most dedicated and inspired cooks I know, for her help in creating many of these low-cholesterol recipes.

Second, I'd like to thank my friends and neighbors who, ever willing to serve as guinea pigs, helped "proof the pudding" during the three years I was developing recipes for this book. They never failed to tell me what they *really* thought, and because of their honest appraisals, I went back to the test kitchen time and again until they agreed I had a "winner."

Third, deepest thanks to photographer Dennis Galante and food stylist Dora Jonassen for making my desserts so Hollywood-glamorous in the photographs, and to friend and colleague Georgia Chan Downard, who also helped prep much of the food for the camera.

Fourth, a *huge* thanks to my agent, Barney Karpfinger, who believed in this project from the start and found it a proper home, and finally, to my ever professional, always available Doubleday editors, John Duff and Judy Kern, who handled both manuscript and author with plenty of "t.l.c."

$\mathcal{C}$ONTENTS

CHAPTER

1

$\mathcal{F}$OREWORD

$\mathcal{A}$s a New York physician who loves to eat, especially sweets, I have enjoyed many of Jean Anderson's creations. I have been most impressed with her integrity and willingness to redo her recipes for this book in view of the recent controversy involving the negative role of trans fatty acids in margarines versus total fat and cholesterol intake. She has now recalculated the fat content of each of these desserts in addition to reducing the cholesterol so that all are consistent with good health, excellent taste, and enjoyability.

$\mathcal{T}$he fact that these recipes are also associated with lowering the "bad" cholesterol and raising the "good" cholesterol is ample evidence of her culinary and scientific background. Miss Anderson has achieved the proper perspective between reality and academia.

Allen W. Mead, M.D.
Internist,
New York Hospital-
Cornell Medical Center
Clinical Associate Professor of Medicine,
Cornell University Medical College

PREFACE

*T*he recipes in Jean Anderson's *Sin-Free Desserts* demonstrate clearly that food that is good for you can taste good too. Here is a cookbook that promotes good heart health while satisfying the American desire for sweet and luscious desserts. As a nutritionist, I applaud Jean's commitment to providing tempting recipes that are low in cholesterol, total fat, saturated fat, and calories.

*F*eeding a family in the 1990s can be challenging. Research has shown that the risk for many of the "killer" diseases such as heart attacks and strokes can be reduced by making healthy food choices. The next step is applying that information to the meals and snacks served. *Sin-Free Desserts* can help health-conscious individuals moderate their intake of cholesterol, fat, and calories because the recipes are complete with relevant nutrient information. These recipes are also appropriate for those persons who are on modified fat and cholesterol diets.

*B*ut that is only part of the picture. For many, dessert is the highlight of the meal. As nutritionists well know, asking people to forgo their favorite sweet in the interests of good health is advice that more often than not falls on deaf ears. But dessert doesn't have to be a nutritional disaster. People can be motivated to make positive dietary changes—and stick to them—if they find substitutes that are appetizing and appealing. And this cookbook is chock full of nutritious replacements. So why not indulge in a low-calorie, low-cholesterol dessert that can make risk reduction a pleasure? It's hard to feel deprived if Steamed Chocolate Hazelnut Pudding, Buttermilk Pound Cake, or Lemon Angel Pie is featured on the menu.

*T*hose who enjoy cooking—and I am one of them—will appreciate the marvelous assortment of recipes offered in *Sin-Free Desserts* as well as the ingenuity of ingredient choices, and the clear and precise instructions. And individuals lucky enough to enjoy the finished products can look forward to glorious desserts that keep their good health in mind.

Barbara B. Deskins, Ph.D., R.D.
Associate Professor
Clinical Dietetics and Nutrition Department
University of Pittsburgh

$\mathcal{I}$NTRODUCTION

$\mathcal{W}$ho among us, given a low-cholesterol life sentence, would dream that we could luxuriate in a sinful Chocolate-Hazelnut Dacquoise without going out of dietary bounds? Or a showy Tipsy Parson? Or a gooey Old-Fashioned Lemon Chess Pie?

$\mathcal{N}$one, probably. And yet we *can* tuck into some of the world's most devastating desserts because it is possible to strip them of their cholesterol—the showy international favorites as well as such homespun "comfort foods" as cheesecake, butterscotch pudding, strawberry shortcake, even pound cake. It takes a bit of culinary alchemy, it's true. But it can be done without sacrificing an ounce of original goodness.

$\mathcal{B}$est of all, lowering the cholesterol in desserts also means reducing the overall fat (*especially saturated fat*) and that's a good policy for all of us. There's an added bonus, too—fewer calories. For example, unsweetened baking chocolate weighs in at 143 calories, 15 grams of fat (much of it saturated) *per ounce*. Not good. But if you substitute unsweetened cocoa powder, as I've done in the recipes that follow, the counts plummet: 1 tablespoon of unsweetened cocoa powder contains about 15 calories and ½ gram of saturated fat. (According to most standard tables of equivalents, 3 tablespoons cocoa powder plus 1 tablespoon fat equal 1 ounce unsweetened chocolate. But I've found that 1 to 1½ tablespoons of a really deep, dark cocoa powder—especially the Dutch process type—are about as chocolaty as a full ounce of solid chocolate. And that's *without* any additional fat.)

$\mathcal{C}$ream cheese and sour cream may be off-limits, but their new vegetable-based doubles trim cholesterol to zero, overall fat by at least ⅓, and saturated fats to less than ½ gram per tablespoon. Heavy cream is taboo, of course, but a little gelatin and ingenuity can make ice creams almost as smooth—and decidedly lower-calorie—than the kind grandmother used to make.

You needn't bypass pastries either when you're watching your cholesterol intake. Monounsaturated olive oil and other polyunsaturated vegetable oils produce respectable piecrusts as do crisp meringues, and graham cracker crumbs tossed with a little olive oil and butter flavor granules. Then, too, turning two-crust pies into open-face tarts is another effective way to lower fat and calories.

You *will* have to skip macadamias and coconut (they're loaded with saturated fats), *but not*, praise be, walnuts, pecans, almonds, and hazelnuts. Used in moderate amounts, these nuts have the power to enrich cakes, cookies, and pies no end without catapulting the grams of fat per serving into the stratosphere (their fats, make a note, are mostly unsaturated). And there are chestnuts, the bulk of whose calories come from carbohydrates, *not* fat.

Egg yolks, of course, are *verboten*, but not the protein-rich whites, which can be whipped into a staggering array of meringues and mousses, soufflés, cakes, even custards--all of them low in fat and cholesterol.

For good heart health, the American Heart Association recommends that we limit our cholesterol intake to 300 milligrams per day. So what, then, *is* a low-cholesterol dessert? Anything below 50 milligrams per serving. And to think that single portions of some butter-, egg-, and cream-rich desserts contain 5 times that amount, not to mention gobs of saturated fats! These fats, according to a recent *Tufts University Diet & Nutrition Letter*, do "more to raise cholesterol levels in the blood than the cholesterol in food."

And what about margarine, so recently indicted by a couple of Dutch scientists? In a study of 59 men and women, they discovered that margarine actually increases the risk of coronary disease instead of reducing it as we, the unsuspecting public, have been led to believe all of these years. The culprits, it turns out, are the "trans fatty acids" formed during the hydrogenation of margarine—the process during which liquid vegetable oils are hardened to the consistency of butter. It also turns out that American food researchers had been wary of these trans fatty acids for some time, too. But it took the Dutch study to pinpoint the specific danger: The trans fatty acids raised the levels of the bad cholesterol in the blood [LDL], which increases the formation of artery-clogging fatty plaques. And in a kind of double-whammy, they also lowered the levels of the good cholesterol [HDL], which flushes the fatty deposits out.

I had no sooner finished developing the recipes for this book than news of this nutritional bombshell spread across the pages of every major American newspaper and magazine. Needless to say, I panicked. Then I began reviewing each of my recipes carefully. A good many of them *did* contain more margarine than I thought wise.

So back to the stove I went—not only to substitute olive or vegetable oil for margarine wherever possible but also to trim overall fat and sugar even more than I had the first time around. You *will* find small amounts of margarine in some of my recipes. But note that it is soft tub or squeeze (liquid) margarine, which contain fewer of the recently incriminated trans fatty acids than stick margarines, also less hydrogenated, thus saturated, fat. You should also note that no physician or dietitian is suggesting that as a result of the Dutch study, you switch back to butter. Far from it. As a highly saturated fat, butter still has "a more damaging effect on blood cholesterol than any margarine," says Dr. Scott M. Grundy of the University of Texas Southwestern Medical Center at Dallas. He further counsels that *all* fats—margarines, oils, whatever—be used in moderation. And that, certainly, was the guideline I used in developing the 150 desserts here.

When I set out to write this cookbook three years ago, *my aim was to bring the cholesterol count of each dessert down to less than 20 milligrams per serving—often far less. Also to reduce the overall amount of fat as much as possible. Still, every dessert had to taste as good as it looked.*

Not easy, I can tell you. It's meant a lot of work, a lot of trial and error, a lot of flops and fizzles along the way. But I was determined to come up with a first-rate collection of low-fat, low-cholesterol desserts that everyone—*dieters and nondieters alike*—would find irresistible.

$\mathcal{I}$ have also tried—and managed—to reduce the sugar content in a good percentage of the recipes, too, because I've always had a sweet tooth—and a weight problem—and yet I feel cheated whenever I must forego dessert. I'm pleased to say that nearly three-fourths of these desserts are genuinely low-calorie: less than 300 calories per serving. To be perfectly honest, you can't whack calories, cholesterol, *and* saturated fats from every dessert and come up with a winner 100 percent of the time. Too many dessert recipes are critical—apt to fail if their proportions are altered too much.

$\mathcal{S}$o, if the calories occasionally soar, it's invariably in a show-stopper party dessert. Have no fear. This once-in-a-blue-moon calorie binge in no way compromises the low-cholesterol or low-saturated-fat counts.

$\mathcal{T}$he aim of this book, then, is to provide cholesterol-counters with the kinds of desserts they thought they could only dream of. *Scores* of them.

$\mathcal{S}$o, dive in, and enjoy with a clear conscience.

Jean Anderson
New York, New York, 1991

ABOUT INGREDIENTS

In General

All measures are standard, all measurements level.

Never substitute one ingredient for another unless the recipe specifies alternate ingredients (oil for margarine, for example; honey for sugar).

And in Particular

Baking Powder: All recipes were tested with double-acting baking powder.

Butter Extract: Before developing the recipes for this book, I must admit that I had never used any "extracts" other than vanilla and almond. But when you're subtracting all butter and most of the margarine from desserts, you need to inject a little butter flavor. I've found butter extract especially effective in cakes when used in conjunction with vanilla.

Butter Flavor Granules: Compounded of maltodextrin (a carbohydrate extracted from corn), partially hydrogenated vegetable oils, lecithin, and such natural colorings as turmeric and annatto, these butter-flavored sprinkles can be used with great success in both baking and stove-top cooking. I've also found that when mixed with a little olive oil, they produce a very butter-like spread—great for those old-fashioned fruit puddings that call for slices or cubes of buttered bread. There are several different butter flavor granules on the market—all in national distribution—but the one I prefer is the not-very-salty Butter Buds (some brands are heavily salted). I've used butter flavor granules in all kinds of recipes throughout this book—in pastries and puddings, cakes and cookies. Usually a tablespoon or so of butter flavor granules is enough to impart a believable butter flavor, but whenever I'm striving for doubly rich butter flavor, I also add a bit of butter extract.

Chocolate: Baking chocolate, whether unsweetened, semisweet, or sweet, contains no cholesterol, but it *is* high in saturated fats, which can raise cholesterol levels in the body. I have therefore relied heavily on unsweetened cocoa powder, which trims the saturated fats by 75 to 80 percent (and even more if you use the lowfat cocoas sold by some groceries and health food stores). I prefer *Dutch process cocoa* because of its depth of flavor. *Sift the cocoa or not as individual recipes direct.*

Cream Cheese Substitute: Formulated from soy bean oil, casein (milk protein), and too many other ingredients to name here, this zero-cholesterol cream cheese look-and-taste-alike is stocked in the dairy counters of many supermarkets. It is not, alas, a low-calorie food—I suppose that's too much to ask. But it does contain 20 percent fewer calories than real cream cheese (80 calories per ounce vs. 100), and more important, it's low in sodium and saturated fats (2 grams per ounce vs. 6 grams for real cream cheese). The brand I used in developing the recipes in this book was Soft Cream Cheese Style Formagg, produced by the Galaxy Cheese Company of New Castle, Pennsylvania. But there are others. Always scrutinize the package label to make sure what you buy is low in saturated fats (no more than 2 grams per ounce) as well as low in cholesterol.

Egg Whites: Unless directed otherwise, use whites from *large eggs.* You'll note that in some recipes I call for both egg whites *and* liquid egg substitute—usually in cakes and soufflés. There's good reason for this. The egg substitute does the job of the yolks, that is, both thickening and binding the basic batter or sauce. The whites are beaten until soft and billowing, then folded into the batter or sauce, which they leaven impressively during baking.

Labna: This is nothing more than yogurt from which all of the intensely acid whey has been drained (see the recipe on page 176). If you use nonfat yogurt, as I do, the creamy curd is just what the doctor ordered. It doubles nicely for whipped cream and cream cheese, and when used in cooking, it's far more stable (less likely to curdle) than yogurt right out of the carton. You'll be amazed at the amount of whey that drains off, but the resulting labna is superbly sweet and silky.

Liquid Egg Substitute: There are a number of these on the market, most of them creamy golden blends of egg whites and polyunsaturated vegetable oils. The one I used in this book was Fleischmann's Egg Beaters, which contains zero fat and cholesterol. It comes frozen and must be thawed thoroughly before it's used. Once thawed, however, it will keep about a week in the refrigerator.

Margarine: There is a lot of confusion about margarine. First of all, margarine is not low in calories. Stick margarine contains 100 calories per tablespoon (99 percent of these from fat)—the same as butter. But there's a difference. Butterfat is animal fat, i.e., highly saturated, and saturated fats can actually do more to raise the level of cholesterol in the blood than the cholesterol present in food. Most margarines are made from relatively unsaturated vegetable oils such as corn or safflower, but these are then partially hydrogenated to give them the consistency of butter. Unfortunately, this process not only saturates some of their fat but also produces trans fatty acids, which according to a recent Dutch study, actually *increase* the risk of heart disease. As I explained in my Introduction (which see), these trans fatty acids both lower the amount of "good cholesterol" in the blood (HDL) and elevate the levels of the "bad" (LDL). All the more reason to substitute mono- or polyunsaturated vegetable oils for margarine or butter. If you must use margarine (and some of my dessert recipes do call for minimal amounts of it), use *unsalted soft tub margarine* or *squeeze (liquid) margarine*, which contain less saturated fats and trans fatty acids than stick margarine (and that goes for greasing pans, too). *Note: Do not substitute the extra-light or "whipped" tub margarine for the regular tub margarine in these recipes, because it has been pumped up with air and/or water and will behave differently in cooking. Read labels!*

Meringue Powder: I had a double handicap while testing recipes for this book. First of all, I had to trim cholesterol, which usually means using plenty of raw beaten egg whites to approximate the fluffiness of whipped cream. But with the recent outbreak of salmonella in the American poultry industry and the danger of food poisoning it poses, it's risky to use raw egg whites (cooked one are completely safe). I solved the problem by calling for an ingredient long known to chefs. It's *meringue powder,* made from dehydrated egg whites, which is packed airtight in 10-ounce lots in plastic containers and needs only to be stored in a cool dry spot. Meringue powder whips to stratospheric heights and can add uncommon creaminess to all manner of mousses. The best source: Maid of Scandinavia, 3244 Raleigh Avenue, Minneapolis, MN 55416. Phone orders accepted: 800-328-6722.

Milk: I've used *evaporated skim milk* often because it has richer flavor and a creamier texture than either fresh lowfat or skim milk. It is also more stable when heated, meaning it's less apt to curdle, and it is singularly compatible with chocolate, caramel, and butterscotch. As for other types of milk, I am quite specific about when to use *nonfat dry milk powder, lowfat buttermilk, fresh skim, or lowfat milk (with either 1 or 2 percent butterfat)*. Only rarely have I called for whole milk, and then only when it was needed to impart essential richness. Use only the type of milk each recipe specifies; make *no* substitutions.

Oils: The oil I like best as a butter/margarine substitute is the *monounsaturated extra-light olive oil* because olive oils are believed to raise blood levels of good cholesterol (HDL) and reduce artery-clogging clumps of fatty substances. I also love the mellow, faintly fruity flavor of the extra-light olive oil and think that it complements most fruits splendidly, not to mention absolutely everything made with chocolate or brown sugar. I can't claim the idea as my own because the Italians and Portuguese have been making cakes with olive oil for centuries. You can, to be sure, substitute any polyunsaturated vegetable oil such as canola, safflower, sunflower, or corn for olive oil, but you should know that some food researchers now suspect that these highly unsaturated oils may be carcinogenic. Is this just more "nutribabble" or a genuine concern? Time will tell.

Sour Cream Substitute: Like cream cheese substitutes, this is a vegetable-based product (corn or soy bean oil plus skim milk solids and plenty of other ingredients). It contains zero cholesterol and less than 1 gram of saturated fat per ounce. At 40 calories per ounce, however, it can scarcely qualify as low-calorie fare (still, that's a third fewer calories than real sour cream). I used two different brands while developing these low-cholesterol recipes: Formagg Sour Cream Style, from the Galaxy Cheese Company of New Castle, Pennsylvania, and King Cholesterol-Free Non Butterfat Sour Cream Alternative, manufactured by American Whipped Products of Newburgh, New York. Both these sour cream substitutes are low in sodium, yet look and taste remarkably like "the real thing." I also found that they held up well during cooking and did not separate any more easily than real sour cream.

Sugar: Whenever two different kinds of sugar are used within a single recipe (granulated sugar, for example, plus brown or confectioners' sugar), both types of sugar are spelled out. Elsewhere, whenever only one kind of sugar is called for, I say simply "sugar" and that means *granulated sugar. Note: Always measure brown sugar firmly packed. Sift confectioners' sugar or not as individual recipes direct.* Do not use any sugar substitutes in place of sugar in any of these recipes.

Yogurt: I am quite specific about the types of yogurt that should be used in each recipe—lowfat, nonfat, or plain yogurt. Do not substitute one for another.

ABOUT NUTRITIVE COUNTS

*F*igures per average-size serving are set down to the nearest round number for calories (148 calories instead of 147.79), for protein (4 grams [g] instead of 4.01), for carbohydrate (30 grams [g] rather than 29.89), and for sodium (61 milligrams [mg] instead of 60.56). But when it comes to the three major concerns of this book—*cholesterol, total fat,* and *saturated fat*—I go into greater detail and show each of them to the first decimal point: 1.5 milligrams [mg] cholesterol, for example, 3.7 grams [g] total fat, and 0.8 grams [g] saturated fat. Finally, whenever portions are small, as in the case of sauces, toppings, and cookies, I show the counts per tablespoon or per piece. There's a good reason for this. You'll rarely confine yourself to a single tablespoon of sauce or a single brownie, and the numbers quickly add up.

*W*henever recipes yield a variable number of servings (i.e., 6 to 8), the first and higher number represents 6 servings, the second and lower number, 8.

Unless otherwise indicated, all nutritive counts are based upon recipe ingredients and do not include optional toppings, garnishes, and sauces.

Abbreviations Used: C (calorie), P (protein), TF (total fat), SAT, (saturated fat), CARB (carbohydrate), S (sodium), CH (cholesterol). Also, g = gram and mg = milligram.

Note: If you are on a low-sodium diet, use only low-sodium or salt-free margarines and other prepared foods.

⚜ = Low-calorie (fewer than 300 calories per serving, and this applies to nearly 75 percent of the recipes in this book).

$\mathscr{J}$EAN

$\mathscr{A}$NDERSON'S

$\mathscr{S}$IN-$\mathscr{F}$REE

$\mathscr{D}$ESSERTS

1

CLAFOUTI, COBBLER, CRÊPES, AND OTHER FRUIT DESSERTS

PEACH CHARLOTTE

MAKES 8 SERVINGS

⚖

2 tablespoons unsalted soft tub margarine (not extra-light)

¼ cup plus 3 tablespoons sugar

2 tablespoons water

1 vanilla bean, split lengthwise

1 tablespoon freshly squeezed lemon juice

2 pounds ripe peaches, peeled, pitted, and coarsely chopped

3 tablespoons extra-light olive oil or vegetable oil (canola, safflower, sunflower, corn oil, etc.) blended with 1 tablespoon butter flavor granules

6 slices firm-textured white bread, crusts removed

PER SERVING: 209 C   2 g P   8.6 g TF
(1 g SAT)   31 g CARB   161 mg S   0.8 mg CH

ℐf fresh peaches aren't available, make this melt-in-your-mouth pudding with nectarines, apricots, or plums.

𝒫reheat the oven to hot (400° F.). Heat the margarine in a large skillet 1 minute over moderate heat. Add the ¼ cup sugar, the water, vanilla bean, and lemon juice and heat, shaking the skillet occasionally, until the sugar dissolves completely. Add the peaches and cook, uncovered, stirring occasionally, for 10 minutes or until almost all liquid has cooked away; set off the heat, scrape the seeds from the vanilla bean into the peaches, and discard the pod.

𝒫lace the oil mixture in a small bowl and the remaining sugar on a saucer. Lightly spray a 6-cup charlotte mold or round-bottomed metal bowl with nonstick vegetable cooking spray, then place 1 bread slice in the bottom. Cut 4 of the remaining slices into dominoes or other shapes as needed to cover the bottom and sides of the mold. Before setting the bread permanently into place, brush one side of each piece with the oil mixture, then press into the sugar. Arrange in the mold so that the sugared sides are against the mold.

𝒮poon the peach mixture into the mold, brush one side of the remaining whole slice of bread with the oil mixture, then press into the sugar, and place, sugared-side-up, on top of the peaches. Cover the mold with foil, set on a baking sheet, and bake 40 minutes in the preheated oven. Carefully remove the foil and bake 20 minutes longer until lightly browned and crisp. Cool the charlotte upright on a wire rack 10 minutes, carefully loosen around the edges with a thin-bladed spatula, and cool upright for 20 minutes longer. Again loosen the charlotte around the edges, then invert onto a small platter. Serve warm or at room temperature.

NECTARINE CLAFOUTI

MAKES 8 SERVINGS

1 pound nectarines, pitted and cut in
½-inch wedges but not peeled
1 teaspoon freshly squeezed lemon juice
1 to 2 tablespoons sugar, as needed to
sweeten the nectarines

BATTER:

¾ cup unsifted all-purpose flour
½ cup firmly packed light brown sugar
½ teaspoon ground cinnamon
⅛ teaspoon ground allspice
⅛ teaspoon salt
1¼ cups lowfat (1 percent) milk
6 tablespoons plain lowfat yogurt
4 egg whites
1 teaspoon vanilla

GLAZE:

2 tablespoons red currant jelly, melted

PER SERVING: 179 C   5 g P   1 g TF
(0.4 g SAT)   37 g CARB   99 mg S   2 mg CH

Try this French country cobbler when nectarines are at their peak of flavor. Try it, too, with fresh peaches and plums.

Preheat the oven to moderately hot (375° F.). Lightly grease a 9-inch pie plate and set aside; toss the nectarines with the lemon juice and sugar and set aside also.

For the Batter: Combine the flour, sugar, cinnamon, allspice, and salt in a medium-size bowl. In a separate bowl, combine the milk, yogurt, egg whites, and vanilla, dump into the dry ingredients, and stir just until no lumps remain.

Pour the batter into the prepared pie plate and arrange the nectarine wedges artfully on top. Bake, uncovered, 30 to 35 minutes in the preheated oven until the batter is set. Cool upright on a wire rack 20 minutes, then brush with the glaze. Cut into wedges and serve warm or at room temperature.

GRATIN OF FRESH RASPBERRIES

MAKES 16 SERVINGS

CRUST:

2⅔ cups graham cracker crumbs

2 tablespoons sugar

1 tablespoon butter flavor granules

½ teaspoon ground ginger

⅛ teaspoon ground cinnamon

⅛ teaspoon freshly grated nutmeg

⅓ cup extra-light olive oil or vegetable oil (canola, safflower, sunflower, corn oil, etc.) blended with 2 tablespoons liquid egg substitute

FILLING:

1¾ cups whole milk

¼ cup evaporated skim milk

½ cup sugar

1½ teaspoons unsalted soft tub margarine (not extra-light)

¾ cup liquid egg substitute

2 teaspoons Grand Marnier

¼ teaspoon very finely grated orange zest

2 pints fresh raspberries of uniform size

You can substitute blueberries, small firm blackberries, or strawberries for the raspberries—good to know because raspberries sometimes cost the earth.

For the Crust: Preheat the oven to moderate (350° F.). Combine all ingredients thoroughly, then pat across the bottom and up the sides of a 12 ½-inch fluted tart tin. Set the tart tin on a baking sheet and bake the crust 10 minutes in the preheated oven. Remove and cool to room temperature.

Meanwhile, Prepare the Filling: Bring the whole milk, evaporated milk, sugar, and margarine to a simmer in a small heavy saucepan over moderate heat. Beat a little of the hot milk mixture into the egg substitute, stir back into the pan, and cook and stir over moderately low heat until the custard thickens enough to coat a metal spoon. This may take as long as 20 minutes, but have patience. If you try to rush things by raising the heat, you risk curdling the custard. As soon as the custard thickens, remove from the heat, strain through a fine sieve into a heatproof bowl, then quick-chill by setting in an ice bath for about 30 minutes. Stir occasionally to prevent a "skin" from forming on the surface of the custard. Mix the Grand Marnier and orange zest into the cooled custard, then spread smoothly over the prepared crust.

Arrange a ring of raspberries, hollows down, around the edge of the filling, right up against the walls of the crust, each berry touching its neighbor. Add a second ring inside and tight up against the first one, again with each berry touching all of its neighbors. Continue adding berries this way until the custard is entirely covered with berries. Preheat the broiler.

```
┌─────────────────────────────────┐
│                                 │
│          TOPPING:               │
│      ───────────────            │
│  ⅓ cup freshly grated Parmesan cheese │
│       3 tablespoons sugar       │
│                                 │
│  PER SERVING: 215 C   5 g P   7.8 g TF   (1 g │
│   SAT)   31 g CARB   225 mg S   5.6 mg CH │
│                                 │
└─────────────────────────────────┘
```

For the Topping: Quickly mix the Parmesan cheese and sugar, and sprinkle evenly over the berries. Set 3 inches from the heat of the preheated broiler and broil 2 to 2 ½ minutes until tipped with brown. Cool the tart 1 full hour before cutting into slim wedges.

BLUEBERRY BUCKLE

MAKES 8 TO 10 SERVINGS

TOPPING:

½ cup sugar

½ cup sifted all-purpose flour

2 teaspoons butter flavor granules

½ teaspoon ground cinnamon

¼ teaspoon freshly grated nutmeg

3 tablespoons extra-light olive oil or vegetable oil (canola, safflower, sunflower, corn oil, etc.)

BATTER:

2 cups sifted all-purpose flour

½ cup sugar

2½ teaspoons baking powder

⅛ teaspoon salt

¼ cup liquid egg substitute

¼ cup skim milk

¼ cup whole milk

¼ cup extra-light olive oil or vegetable oil (canola, safflower, sunflower, corn oil, etc.)

1 pint fresh blueberries, stemmed

PER SERVING: 368–295 C   5–4 g P
13–10.5 g TF   (1.9–1.5 g SAT)   59–47 g
CARB   231–185 mg S   1.4–1.1 mg CH

This recipe for a 3-layer Down East cobbler is genuinely old. For best results, use fresh blueberries. Many commercially frozen blueberries are packed in too much sugar to produce an entirely successful buckle, but if you manage to find a package of frozen unsweetened blueberries (now becoming more widely available), by all means use them—still solidly frozen. So that you can whisk the buckle into the oven as soon as you've mixed the batter, prepare the topping first.

Preheat the oven to moderately hot (375° F.). Spray a 9 × 9 × 2-inch baking pan with nonstick vegetable cooking spray and set aside.

For the Topping: Combine the sugar, flour, butter granules, cinnamon, and nutmeg in a small mixing bowl, then fork the oil in, 1 tablespoon at a time, tossing well after each addition until the mixture is uniformly crumbly. Set aside.

For the Batter: Combine the flour, sugar, baking powder, and salt in a large mixing bowl and make a well in the center. Whisk the liquid egg substitute, skim milk, whole milk, and oil together in a large measuring cup, pour into the well in the dry ingredients, and beat just until combined. The batter will be very stiff. Do not overmix or the buckle will be tough. Spread the batter in the bottom of the prepared pan, cover with the blueberries, then scatter the topping evenly over the berries.

Bake the buckle, uncovered, about 1¼ hours in the preheated oven until lightly browned and springy-firm to the touch. If you'd like a browner top, transfer the buckle to the broiler, setting it 4 inches from the heat, and broil 1 to 2 minutes until tipped with brown. Remove from the oven and cool the buckle upright in its pan for 30 minutes before serving. Cut into large squares and serve as is, or drift with Mock Whipped Cream (page 174).

BLUEBERRY FUNGI

MAKES 6 TO 8 SERVINGS

8 slices firm-textured white bread
4 tablespoons unsalted soft tub
margarine (not extra-light)
1 quart fresh blueberries, stemmed
1 cup sugar

PER SERVING: 337–252 C   3–2.5 g P   8.9–
6.6 g TF   (1.6–1.2 g SAT)   63–47 g
CARB   168–126 mg S   0.9–0.7 mg CH

This French-Canadian dessert couldn't be easier to make, but you must use fresh blueberries. And what's the origin of the unusual title? No one I queried, and no amount of digging in the library, could provide an answer.

Preheat the oven to moderate (350° F.). Spray a 9 × 9 × 2-inch baking pan with nonstick vegetable cooking spray and set aside.

Spread each slice of bread well with margarine—one side only—then arrange 4 slices, spread-sides-up, in the prepared baking pan. Spoon ½ the blueberries on top and sprinkle with ½ the sugar. Using a potato masher, press the blueberries firmly to crush lightly. Arrange the remaining bread slices, spread-sides-up, on top of the blueberries, cover with the remaining blueberries, and sprinkle with the remaining sugar. Again crush lightly with a potato masher.

Bake, uncovered, 40 minutes in the preheated oven. Remove the pan from the oven, again press the surface with the potato masher, crushing the berries still further. Return to the oven and bake 10 to 20 minutes longer until the blueberries are syrupy and bubbly. Remove from the oven and cool 20 to 30 minutes before serving.

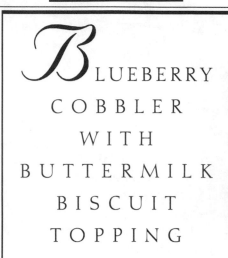

BLUEBERRY COBBLER WITH BUTTERMILK BISCUIT TOPPING

MAKES 6 SERVINGS

FILLING:

5 cups fresh or frozen unsweetened
blueberries (about 1½ pounds)

⅔ cup sugar

2 tablespoons cornstarch

⅛ teaspoon freshly ground black pepper

1 tablespoon sherry wine vinegar

1 teaspoon finely grated lemon zest

BISCUIT TOPPING:

1 cup unsifted all-purpose flour

¼ cup sugar

1 teaspoon baking powder

½ teaspoon baking soda

¼ teaspoon salt

3 tablespoons frozen unsalted soft tub
margarine (not extra-light), diced

½ cup lowfat buttermilk

PER SERVING: 328 C   4 g P   6 g TF   (1 g
SAT)   66 g CARB   258 mg S   0.8 mg CH

There's nothing off-limits for cholesterol-counters in this homey cobbler, which substitutes margarine for lard and lowfat buttermilk for whole milk.

Preheat the oven to hot (425° F.); lightly spray a 9-inch round cake pan with nonstick vegetable cooking spray and set aside.

For the Filling: Place the blueberries in a medium-size heavy suacepan; combine the sugar, cornstarch, and pepper; sprinkle over the berries and stir to coat. Mix in the vinegar and lemon zest, set, uncovered, over moderate heat, bring to a boil, then boil 1 minute. Pour the berry mixture into the prepared pan.

For the Biscuit Topping: Combine the flour, sugar, baking powder, soda, and salt in a medium-size mixing bowl. Scatter the bits of margarine on top and, using a pastry blender, cut the margarine into the dry ingredients until they are the texture of coarse meal. Make a well in the center and pour in the buttermilk. Stir briskly just until the mixture holds together. Turn the dough out onto a lightly floured board and pat to a thickness of ½ inch. Using a floured 2½-inch biscuit cutter, cut the dough into 9 rounds and place on top of the blueberry mixture.

Bake, uncovered, in the preheated oven for 15 to 20 minutes or until the topping is golden brown and the berries bubble. Serve warm.

"SUMMER" PUDDING

MAKES 6 SERVINGS

10 slices firm-textured white bread

½ (12-ounce) package frozen
unsweetened raspberries, thawed and
drained very well

½ (12-ounce) package frozen
unsweetened blueberries, thawed and
drained very well

½ (12-ounce) package frozen
unsweetened pitted dark, sweet red
cherries, thawed and drained very well

⅔ cup sugar

1 tablespoon freshly squeezed lemon
juice

¾ cup diced bread trimmings (from the
slices used to line the pudding mold)

1 recipe Mock Whipped Cream (page
174)

PER SERVING: (WITH 3 TABLESPOONS
MOCK WHIPPED CREAM): 258 C   5 g P
2 g IF   (0.4 g SAT)   57 g CARB
215 mg S   1.6 mg CH

I've put quotes around "summer" because I make this popular English dessert with frozen fruits so that I can enjoy it year round. It's superb, of course, made with a mixture of fresh summer berries—raspberries, blueberries, red currants, even blackberries. You will need about 3 pounds of them in all, well washed, sorted, and stemmed. Heat them with the sugar and lemon juice and proceed as directed, but omit the diced bread trimmings. Frozen berries give off so much juice that the trimmings are needed to thicken them. This dessert must stand in the refrigerator 24 hours before it's served, so plan accordingly.

*G*rease a round-bottomed, 1-quart metal mixing bowl well with unsalted margarine and set aside. Trim the crusts from the bread and reserve. Press a slice of bread flat in the bottom of the bowl, then line the sides with additional slices, pressing them to fit the contours of the bowl and piecing as needed so that no metal shows. Set the bowl aside.

*P*lace all of the berries, the cherries, the sugar, and the lemon juice in a medium-size nonmetallic saucepan, set over moderate heat, and heat, stirring occasionally, 3 to 4 minutes until the sugar dissolves completely. Stir the bread trimmings into the berries, and ladle into the bread-lined bowl. Now fashion a "top," 2 layers thick, by cutting and piecing the remaining bread slices. No berries should show. Place a small flat plate on top of the bread (it should just fit inside the bowl and cover the bread completely), weight with a heavy, unopened can of food, and refrigerate 24 hours.

*W*hen ready to serve, carefully loosen the pudding with a thin-bladed spatula and invert onto a small serving plate. To serve, cut into wedges. Pass the Mock Whipped Cream separately.

STRAWBERRY SHORTCAKE

MAKES 8 SERVINGS

SHORTCAKE:

1⅔ cups sifted all-purpose flour

⅓ cup sugar

1½ teaspoons baking powder

½ teaspoon baking soda

⅔ cup lowfat buttermilk

¼ cup extra-light olive oil or vegetable oil (canola, safflower, sunflower, corn oil, etc.)

FILLING:

1½ teaspoons unflavored gelatin

2 tablespoons cold water

2 cups lowfat (1 percent) cottage cheese

⅓ cup sugar

1 teaspoon vanilla

⅛ teaspoon freshly grated nutmeg

BERRIES:

2 pints strawberries, hulled and halved

¼ cup sugar

2 tablespoons freshly squeezed orange juice

A fluffy cottage cheese filling takes the place of the cholesterol-laden whipped cream we're all used to.

*P*reheat the oven to hot (425° F.). Spray 2 (8-inch) round cake pans with nonstick vegetable cooking spray and set aside.

For the Shortcake: Sift the flour, sugar, baking powder, and soda into a medium-size mixing bowl and make a well in the center. Combine the buttermilk and oil, pour into the well, and mix briskly just enough to make a soft but manageable dough; do not overmix or the shortcake will be tough.

*W*ith lightly floured hands, pat the dough over the bottom of the prepared pans in a thin layer, dividing the total amount equally. Bake 12 minutes in the preheated oven until golden brown and a toothpick inserted in the center comes out clean. Cool the shortcakes in the upright pans on wire racks 10 minutes, then invert on the racks and cool completely.

Meanwhile, Prepare the Filling: Combine the gelatin and water in a heatproof ramekin and let stand 5 minutes. Stand the ramekin in a small pan of hot water, set over moderately low heat, and heat 3 to 4 minutes until the gelatin dissolves completely; set aside. Churn the cottage cheese, sugar, vanilla, and nutmeg in a food processor fitted with the metal chopping blade 1 to 1½ minutes until smooth. Add the gelatin and churn 20 seconds; transfer to a medium-size bowl, cover, and refrigerate 30 minutes.

For the Berries: Purée ½ the berries, the sugar, and orange juice by churning 1 minute in a food processor fitted with the metal chopping blade. Transfer to a medium-size bowl, add the remaining berries, and toss well.

*2 tablespoons confectioners' sugar (for
dusting)*
4 perfect whole strawberries

PER SERVING: 310 C   11 g P   8 g TF   (1 g
SAT)   48 g CARB   384 mg S   3 mg CH

To Assemble the Shortcake: Place 1 shortcake on a serving platter, spoon the cottage-cheese filling on top, then ⅔ of the berry mixture. Cut the second shortcake into 8 wedges of equal size and arrange them in a circle on top. Ladle the remaining berry mixture over all, then dust, if you like, with confectioners' sugar and garnish with the whole berries.

CARAMELIZED FRESH PEAR PUDDING

MAKES 6 SERVINGS

FOR CARAMELIZING THE MOLD:

⅓ cup sugar

¼ cup plus 1 tablespoon water

1 teaspoon freshly squeezed lemon juice

2 tablespoons unsalted soft tub margarine (not extra-light)

½ cup fine soft bread crumbs

PEAR MIXTURE:

1¼ pounds ripe pears, peeled, cored, and sliced thin

⅓ cup water

2 tablespoons sugar

1 tablespoon freshly squeezed lemon juice

¼ teaspoon ground ginger

2 (2 × ½-inch) strips lemon zest

CUSTARD:

3 egg whites, lightly beaten

1 cup whole milk

6 tablespoons sugar

⅛ teaspoon ground cinnamon

⅛ teaspoon ground ginger

⅛ teaspoon salt

PER SERVING: 237 C   4 g P   5 g TF   (1.5 g SAT)   45 g CARB   113 mg S   5.8 mg CH

Delicious hot or cold.

To Caramelize the Mold: Combine the sugar, the ¼ cup water, and the lemon juice in a small heavy saucepan; set, uncovered, over moderate heat, and cook 4 to 5 minutes without stirring until pale amber. Carefully add the 1 tablespoon water to the pan, swirl it around, and pour the caramel mixture over the bottom and slightly up the sides of a 4- to 6-cup charlotte mold or soufflé dish. Spray any uncaramelized parts on the inside of the mold with nonstick vegetable cooking spray. Melt the margarine in a small heavy skillet over moderate heat, add the bread crumbs, and cook, tossing occasionally, about 5 minutes until golden. Scatter the crumbs over the caramel mixture in the bottom of the mold.

For the Pear Mixture: Place the pears, water, sugar, lemon juice, ginger, and lemon zest in a medium-size heavy saucepan and set over moderately low heat. Cover and cook, stirring occasionally, about 30 minutes until the mixture is reduced to a thick sauce (the timing will depend on the ripeness of the fruit). Discard the lemon zest, then spoon the pear mixture on top of the bread crumbs.

For the Custard: Preheat the oven to moderately slow (325° F.). Whisk the egg whites, milk, sugar, cinnamon, ginger, and salt in a small bowl until well combined. Pour over the pears.

Bake, uncovered, 30 to 35 minutes in the preheated oven or until a toothpick inserted halfway between the rim and the center comes out clean. Cool the pudding upright in its pan for 10 minutes, then loosen around the edge and invert on a serving plate with a rim (to catch the juices). Serve hot or at room temperature.

BUCKWHEAT CRÊPES WITH CRANBERRY-STRAWBERRY FILLING

MAKES 4 SERVINGS

CRÊPES:

6 tablespoons unsifted all-purpose flour

3 tablespoons unsifted buckwheat or
whole wheat flour

1 tablespoon sugar

1½ egg whites, lightly beaten

¾ cup lowfat (1 percent) milk

FILLING:

1 pint strawberries, hulled and
moderately thinly sliced

1½ cups cranberries, stemmed and sorted

⅔ cup sugar

1 vanilla bean, split lengthwise

TOPPINGS AND GARNISH:

3 tablespoons confectioners' sugar

1 cup plain lowfat yogurt

4 perfect strawberries

PER SERVING: 359 C 8 g P 4.8 g TF (1.4 g
SAT) 72 g CARB 85 mg S 5.2 mg CH

The easiest way to measure ½ an egg white is to beat 1 whole egg white until frothy, measure the total amount, then remove ½ of it (save the remaining ½ white for a soup or sauce).

For the Crêpes: Combine the flours and sugar in a medium-size bowl, whisk in the egg whites and milk, and beat until well combined. Lightly grease an 8-inch nonstick skillet with margarine, set over moderately high heat, and when the pan is hot—after about 1 minute—add a scant 3 tablespoons of crêpe batter. Swirl the pan until the batter coats the skillet bottom. Cook about 1 minute until set, turn the crêpe, and cook the flip side 20 seconds. Repeat with the remaining batter, placing the finished crêpes on a plate, separated by sheets of wax paper. You should have 8 crêpes.

For the Filling: Mix the strawberries, cranberries, sugar, and vanilla bean in a medium-size heavy saucepan and bring to a boil over moderate heat. Adjust the heat so the mixture bubbles gently, then simmer, uncovered, about 10 minutes until all the cranberries have popped and the mixture is as thick as applesauce (you should have 2 cups). Scrape the seeds from the vanilla bean into the mixture and discard the pod.

To Assemble: Spread each crêpe with ¼ cup of the filling, leaving a 1-inch border all around. Fold the right and left sides in toward the middle, then roll the crêpes up jelly-roll style. Place 2 filled crêpes on each of 4 dessert plates and dust with confectioners' sugar, using 1 tablespoon in all. Combine the remaining confectioners' sugar with the yogurt and add a dollop to each plate, spooning it to one side of the crêpes. Slice each strawberry from tip to the stem, almost but not all the way through the stem end, then spread the slices into a fan. Add a strawberry fan to each plate and serve.

APPLE CRÊPE STACK CAKE

MAKES AN 8-INCH CAKE, 6 TO 8
SERVINGS

APPLESAUCE FILLING:

2 pounds assorted cooking apples
(Greenings, McIntosh, Granny Smiths,
etc.)
⅓ cup firmly packed light brown sugar
⅓ cup granulated sugar
¼ cup water
6 whole cloves
6 whole allspice
4 (2 × ½-inch) strips orange zest
1 vanilla bean, split lengthwise
1 cinnamon stick, split lengthwise (this
releases more flavor)

CRÊPES:

½ cup unsifted all-purpose flour
¼ cup unsifted buckwheat or whole
wheat flour
1½ tablespoons granulated sugar
2 eggs whites, lightly beaten
1 cup plus 1 tablespoon lowfat
(1 percent) milk

This is a low-cholesterol version of a dessert made at Brandywine's, an Alsatian restaurant in the Gramercy Park district of New York City. And it's every bit as good as the original.

For the Applesauce Filling: Wash but do not peel or core the apples; slice thin and place in a large heavy saucepan with all remaining filling ingredients. Set, uncovered, over moderate heat and bring to a boil; adjust the heat so mixture bubbles gently, cover, and simmer, stirring occasionally, about 40 minutes until the apples are mushy. *Note: If at any point the apples are in danger of scorching, add a little more water.* Dump the hot apple mixture into a food mill and push it through; discard the skin and other solids left behind. Return the applesauce to the pan and cook, uncovered, over moderate heat until reduced to 2¼ cups—about 10 minutes. Set aside.

For the Crêpes: Combine the flours and sugar in a medium-size bowl, whisk in the egg whites and milk, and beat until well combined. Lightly grease an 8-inch nonstick skillet with margarine, set over moderately high heat, and when the pan is good and hot—after about 1 minute—add a scant 3 tablespoons of crêpe batter and swirl the pan until the batter coats the skillet bottom. Cook about 1 minute until set, turn the crêpe and cook the flip side 20 seconds. Repeat with the remaining batter, placing the finished crêpes on a plate and separating one from the other with a sheet of wax paper. You should have 10 crêpes.

NUT MIXTURE:

---

3 tablespoons ground unblanched almonds

3 tablespoons dry bread crumbs

2 tablespoons granulated sugar

TOPPING:

---

1 tablespoon confectioners' sugar (for dusting)

<u>PER SERVING</u>: 308–231 C   5–4 g P   2.9–2.2 g TF   (0.6–0.4 g SAT)   68–51 g CARB   67–51 mg S   1.9–1.4 mg CH

For the Nut Mixture: Mix all ingredients and set aside. Preheat the oven to moderately hot (375° F.). Lightly spray an 8-inch round baking pan at least 1½ inches deep with nonstick vegetable cooking spray. Now sprinkle the pan lightly with a little of the nut mixture.

To Assemble: Lay a crêpe on top, sprinkle lightly with a little more of the nut mixture, then spread with ¼ cup of the applesauce filling. Continue the layering until you have used up 8 more crêpes and all of the apple and nut mixtures. Top with the remaining crêpe.

Cover with foil and bake 15 minutes in the preheated oven. Remove from the oven, cool to room temperature, then refrigerate for at least 1 hour before serving. Remove the foil, invert the stack cake on a serving plate, and dust with confectioners' sugar. To serve, cut into wedges.

HONEY-YOGURT-BLUEBERRY CRÊPES

MAKES 4 SERVINGS

CRÊPES:

9 tablespoons unsifted all-purpose flour
4 teaspoons sugar
¼ teaspoon ground ginger
Pinch of salt
1½ egg whites, lightly beaten (see headnote, page 15)
¾ cup lowfat (1 percent) milk

FILLING:

1 cup plain lowfat yogurt
¼ cup honey
1 pint blueberries, stemmed
½ teaspoon vanilla
⅛ teaspoon freshly ground black pepper

TOPPING:

1 tablespoon confectioners' sugar (for dusting)

PER SERVING: 281 C 8 g P 4.6 g TF
(1.4 g SAT) 54 g CARB 122 mg S 5.2 mg CH

For the Crêpes: Combine the flour, sugar, ginger, and salt in a medium-size bowl, whisk in the egg whites and milk, and beat until well combined. Lightly grease an 8-inch nonstick skillet with margarine, set over moderately high heat, and when the pan is good and hot—after about 1 minute—add a scant 3 tablespoons of crêpe batter and swirl the pan until the batter coats the skillet bottom. Cook about 1 minute until set, turn the crêpe, and cook the flip side 20 seconds. Repeat with the remaining batter, placing the finished crêpes on a plate and separating one from the other with a sheet of wax paper. You should have 8 crêpes.

For the Filling: Combine the yogurt and honey in a 2-cup measure, then mix ½ this mixture with the blueberries, vanilla, and pepper. Reserve the remaining yogurt-honey mixture.

To Assemble: Spoon a scant ⅓ cup of the blueberry filling in the center of each crêpe, leaving a 1-inch border all around. Fold the right and left sides in toward the middle, then roll the crêpes up jelly-roll style. Place 2 filled crêpes on each of 4 dessert plates and dust with confectioners' sugar. Spoon the remaining yogurt-honey mixture over each portion and serve.

ROTE GRÜTZE

MAKES 8 SERVINGS

ROTE GRÜTZE:

2 (10-ounce) packages frozen raspberries, thawed, with their juice

1 (16-ounce) package frozen strawberries, thawed, with their juice

1 (1-pound) can pitted dark, sweet cherries, drained (reserve liquid)

1 quart cranberry juice (about)

⅔ cup sugar

1 tablespoon finely grated orange zest

1 tablespoon finely grated lemon zest

¼ cup freshly squeezed lemon juice

⅔ cup unsifted cornstarch

1 cup dry red wine

TOPPING:

1 cup plain nonfat yogurt

2 tablespoons confectioners' sugar

1 teaspoon vanilla

PER SERVING: 295 C   3 g P   1 g TF   (0 g SAT)   80 g CARB   28 mg S   0.5 mg CH

This German dessert, traditionally made with the red berries of summer, will be better if you make it one day and serve it the next (leftovers, by the way, keep splendidly for several days). I like Rote Grütze so much that I've worked out a year-round version that substitutes frozen berries for the fresh, and I promise you it's as good as the long-winded original.

For the Rote Grütze: Drain the liquid from the raspberries into a 1-quart measuring cup and set the raspberries aside. Put the strawberries and their liquid through a food mill and add to the measure along with the liquid drained from the canned cherries. Now add enough of the cranberry juice to total 1 quart. Pour into a large heavy nonmetallic saucepan and add another 2 cups cranberry juice. Mix in the sugar, orange and lemon zests, and the lemon juice, set over moderate heat, and bring to a boil, stirring frequently. Meanwhile, combine the cornstarch with the wine to make a smooth paste. As soon as the berry mixture boils, whisk in the cornstarch mixture. Reduce the heat to low and cook and whisk 3 minutes—just until the mixture bubbles up, thickens, and clears. Stir in the cherries and reserved raspberries and cook and stir 1 minute longer. Cool to room temperature, then mound in individual goblets and chill 8 hours or overnight.

For the Topping: Combine all ingredients in a small bowl, cover, and chill until ready to serve.

Just before serving, drift each portion of Rote Grütze with some of the topping.

RASPBERRY-STRAWBERRY VACHERIN

MAKES 16 SERVINGS

FOR PREPARING THE BAKING SHEETS:

1½ tablespoons unsalted soft tub margarine (not extra-light)
3 tablespoons all-purpose flour

MERINGUE 1:

6 extra-large egg whites
1¾ cups sugar

MERINGUE 2:

1 cup sugar
½ cup cold water
4 extra-large egg whites

RASPBERRY-STRAWBERRY CRÈME CHANTILLY:

¾ cup cold water
2 envelopes unflavored gelatin
2½ cups unsifted confectioners' sugar
3 cups lowfat (1 percent) cottage cheese
1½ cups no-cholesterol vegetable-based sour cream substitute (see page xix)
1 tablespoon framboise (raspberry liqueur) or kirsch
3 pints ripe strawberries, hulled and thinly sliced

A true vacherin (a meringue basket filled with fresh, fruity crème chantilly) is made with gobs of whipped cream. The party-perfect extravaganza here substitutes a fluffy almost zero-cholesterol look-and-taste-alike. It's thickened with gelatin but sets softly, rather than firmly, like a chiffon pie, so it isn't as neat to serve. The best plan: let your guests "ohh" and "aah" over your finished vacherin, then retreat to the kitchen to cut it. Note: For best results, beat meringues with an electric mixer that has a wire whip attachment. Also, choose a dry sunny day because only then will your meringue basket be crisp (if you store it airtight, you can make it a week ahead of time). Finally, do not fill the meringue basket until you are ready to serve it.

*P*reheat the oven to its keep-warm setting (200° to 250° F.). Grease 3 baking sheets well, using ½ tablespoon margarine for each. Sift 1 tablespoon flour over each sheet, tilt first to one side, then another, until covered with a thin, even film of flour. Tap the excess flour from each baking sheet. Using an 8-inch round cake pan as a guide, draw a circle in the middle of 1 baking sheet. You want to make rows of meringue ladyfingers on the remaining 2 baking sheets, so draw guidelines on these pans for 4-inch ladyfingers, spacing them 1 inch apart. Set all baking sheets aside.

For Meringue 1: Beat the egg whites until frothy in an electric mixer at moderately slow speed, then with the mixer running, add the sugar, 1 tablespoon at a time, pausing 5 seconds between additions. When ½ the sugar has been added, raise the mixer speed to medium and add the remaining sugar, a tablespoon at a time as before; then beat the meringue 5 minutes at highest mixer speed until very thick and glossy but not dry. When you cut through the meringue with a knife, the slash should be clean and crisp.

3 (12-ounce) packages frozen
unsweetened raspberries, thawed and
drained very well (use the raspberry
juice in a fruit drink or pour over cereal)

TOPPINGS AND GARNISHES:

½ pint medium-size raspberries

3 perfect strawberries

4 to 5 small rosettes baked Meringue 2
(optional)

1 sprig lemon or rose geranium, lemon
verbena, or mint

PER SERVING: 332 C   10 g P   3 g TF
(0.5 g SAT.)   73 g CARB   187 mg S
1.9 mg CH

Spoon the meringue into a pastry bag fitted with a plain round tip at least ½ inch in diameter and make a dot in the center of the circle on the prepared baking sheet. Then, beginning at that dot and using firm, steady pressure, coil a line of meringue tightly around and around until you reach the outer edge of the circle; set this baking sheet aside. Now pipe 4 × 1½-inch ladyfingers in the rows you marked on the other baking sheets, spacing them about 1 inch apart. The easiest way to do this is to make elongated U's, with the 2 lines of meringue touching one another.

Bake the meringues 1½ to 2 hours in the preheated oven until firm and crisp but still white (unless you have 2 ovens or an oversize one, you can bake only 2 sheets at a time; keep the third refrigerated). Be sure to reverse the positions of the baking sheets once or twice during baking so that the meringues cook evenly. Remove the meringues from the oven but do not turn the oven off. Cool the meringues to room temperature.

For Meringue 2: Combine the sugar and water in a small heavy saucepan, insert a candy thermometer, set over moderately low heat, and, without stirring, heat to 240° F. If the syrup crystallizes on the sides of the pan, wash down gently with a wet pastry brush. When the syrup approaches 240° F., beat the egg whites to soft peaks in an electric mixer at moderately slow speed. Raise the speed to medium and drizzle in the hot syrup. When all the syrup has been incorporated, beat at highest mixer speed 2 to 3 minutes longer until very stiff and glossy. This is the meringue you will use to "glue" your meringue basket together and also to decorate it.

To Make the Meringue Basket: Place the baked meringue circle on an ungreased baking sheet. Spoon about ½ of Meringue 2 into a large pastry tube fitted with a medium star tip and pipe a thick ring about 1 inch wide and 1 inch deep around the edge of the baked meringue circle. Now build a little picket fence of upended ladyfingers around the edge of the circle, standing them in the soft meringue ring and "gluing" one to the other with a little of the extra Meringue 2. You will use about 16 meringue ladyfingers in all; store any extra ones airtight and serve as cookies another day.

Now pipe a decorative squiggle of meringue down each seam to hide any messy edges, apply rosettes at the top of each meringue ladyfinger, pipe a scalloped border around the base of the meringue basket and, if you like, add a swag around the middle. You'll have a bit more meringue than you need, but no problem. Simply pipe the balance into small rosettes on a greased and floured baking sheet and bake along with the meringue basket (some of these can be used to garnish the *vacherin*, if you like; the rest can be stored airtight and kept for several weeks—they make dainty little cookies). Scoop any excess soft meringue from the inside of the basket, then bake the meringue basket in the preheated oven 2½ to 3 hours until very crisp and dry but still white.

Meanwhile, Prepare the Raspberry-Strawberry Crème Chantilly: Place the water in a very small heavy saucepan, sprinkle the gelatin evenly on top, and let stand 5 minutes. Set the pan over moderately low heat and cook and stir 4 to 5 minutes until the gelatin dissolves completely; set aside. Beat the sugar, cottage cheese, sour cream substitute, and framboise in the large electric mixer bowl at highest speed until smooth and fluffy. Drizzle in the hot gelatin, beating all the while. Fold in the strawberries and raspberries, cover, and chill until ready to use.

To Assemble the Vacherin: Spoon the crème chantilly into the meringue basket, top with the whole raspberries, arranging as artfully as possible. Trim with the perfect strawberries and, if you like, the meringue rosettes, tuck in the sprig of lemon geranium and carry into the dining room for guests to admire. To serve, cut between each of the meringue ladyfingers. Arrange pieces of meringue as attractively as possible in dessert dishes, top with some of the crème chantilly and a few whole berries.

PAVLOVA

MAKES 12 TO 14 SERVINGS

FOR PREPARING THE BAKING SHEET:

½ tablespoon unsalted soft tub margarine (not extra-light)

1 tablespoon all-purpose flour

MERINGUE

5 extra-large egg whites

¾ cup superfine sugar

1 cup sifted confectioners' sugar

1 teaspoon vanilla

½ teaspoon almond extract

FILLING:

½ cup cold water

2 envelopes unflavored gelatin

2 cups lowfat (1 percent) cottage cheese

1 cup plain nonfat yogurt

1 cup unsifted confectioners' sugar

1½ teaspoons vanilla

½ teaspoon almond extract

*T*his Australian classic, named for the prima ballerina Anna Pavlova, is a tutu-frilly meringue basket mounded with whipped cream and fresh fruits. Clearly no cholesterol-counter should indulge in the real thing, but he can enjoy this version without the slightest twinge of guilt because a fluffy cottage-cheese-based filling doubles nicely for the whipped cream. Don't attempt this dessert in humid weather because the meringue won't crisp properly. And to keep the meringue basket from going soggy, don't fill it until just before serving. The natural juices of the fruit will also seep into the cream filling and thin it, making this low-cholesterol Pavlova difficult to serve neatly. No problem. Simply present the finished dessert to dinner guests to admire, then withdraw to the kitchen to portion out the meringue, fruits, and filling.

*P*reheat the oven to its keep-warm setting (200° to 250° F.). Grease a baking sheet well with the margarine, sift the flour over the sheet, and tilt first to one side, then another, until covered with a thin, even film of flour. Tap the excess flour from the baking sheet. Using a casserole or platter as a guide, draw a 9 × 12-inch oval in the middle of the baking sheet; set aside.

For the Meringue: Beat the egg whites until frothy in an electric mixer at moderately slow speed (preferably one with a wire whip attachment); then, with the mixer running, add the superfine sugar, 1 tablespoon at a time, pausing 5 seconds between additions. Raise the mixer speed to medium and add the confectioners' sugar, a rounded tablespoon at a time. Sprinkle the vanilla and almond extract over the meringue, then beat 5 minutes at highest mixer speed until very thick and glossy but not dry. When you cut through the meringue with a knife, the slash should be clean and crisp. Spread ⅔ of the meringue into an oval ¾ inch thick on the baking sheet, pushing the excess meringue to the edge of the oval and using it to build up the sides of the meringue basket to

FRUITS:

2 medium-size ripe nectarines or peaches (about ½ pound), peeled, pitted, sliced thin, and dipped in lemon juice to prevent darkening

2 medium-size kiwi fruits (about ¼ pound), peeled and sliced thin

2 small bananas (about ½ pound), peeled, sliced thin, and dipped in lemon juice to prevent darkening

½ pint medium-size strawberries, hulled, sliced thin, and if too tart, tossed with 1 tablespoon superfine sugar

PER SERVING: 209–179 C   9–8 g P   1–0.9 g TF   (0.4–0.3) g SAT   42–36 g CARB   196–168 mg S   1.9–1.5 mg CH

a height of about 1½ inches. Spoon the remaining meringue into a pastry bag fitted with a large star tip and pipe a row of rosettes around the top of the basket, then a second row around the outside of the base. Bake the meringue basket in the preheated oven 2½ to 3 hours until crisp and dry but still white. Cool about 2 hours or until room temperature in the turned-off oven before filling.

Meanwhile, Prepare the Filling: Place the water in a very small heavy saucepan, sprinkle the gelatin evenly on top, and let stand 5 minutes. Set the pan over moderately low heat and cook and stir 4 to 5 minutes until the gelatin dissolves completely; set aside. Churn all remaining filling ingredients in a food processor fitted with the metal chopping blade 1 to 1½ minutes until absolutely smooth. Add the hot gelatin in a fine stream, pulsing all the while. Transfer to a large mixing bowl (preferably metal), cover, and chill about 1 hour until the mixture mounds nicely on a spoon and does not flatten.

To Assemble the Pavlova: Place the meringue basket on a large platter, spoon in the filling, and smooth over the bottom of the basket. Quickly drain the fruits and arrange on top of the filling in as decorative a pattern as possible—in wedges, alternating the colors, in concentric rings, anything you fancy as long as it's showy. Serve at once, making sure that everyone gets a nice chunk of the meringue basket as well as generous ladlings of fruits and filling.

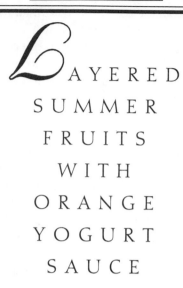

Layered Summer Fruits with Orange Yogurt Sauce

MAKES 12 TO 14 SERVINGS

SAUCE:

1½ cups plain lowfat yogurt

½ cup no-cholesterol vegetable-based sour cream substitute (see page xix)

1 teaspoon finely grated orange zest

2 tablespoons superfine sugar

FRUITS:

1 small very ripe pineapple (1½ to 2 pounds)

6 tablespoons superfine sugar

1 tablespoon coarsely chopped fresh mint

1 quart strawberries, hulled and sliced about ¼ inch thick

1 tablespoon Cointreau or Grand Marnier

2 pounds very ripe peaches or nectarines, peeled, pitted, and cut into slim wedges

For this showy party dessert, the sauce and fruits can all be prepared several hours ahead of time. Keep them in separate covered bowls in the refrigerator and assemble the dessert just before serving. If the different fruits are to be clearly visible, it's best to layer them in a deep glass or crystal bowl. I find that a giant brandy snifter works perfectly.

Prepare the Sauce First: Whisk all ingredients together in a small bowl, cover, and let stand at room temperature until needed.

For the Fruits: Peel the pineapple, quarter lengthwise, then halve each quarter lengthwise so that you have 8 long slim wedges. Slice the point off each wedge to remove the woody core, then slice each wedge crosswise ⅛ inch thick into little "fans" and place in a large bowl. Add 1 tablespoon of the sugar and the mint and toss well; set aside. Place the strawberries in another bowl, add the Cointreau and 2 tablespoons of the sugar. Toss well and set aside. In a third bowl toss the peaches with the lemon juice and remaining sugar and set aside.

To Assemble: Place the grapes in the bottom of a very large, deep glass or crystal bowl. Add the peaches and about ⅓ of the sauce. Add ½ the blueberries, then all the pineapple, and top with another ⅓ of the sauce, letting it trickle down over the fruits below. Next add all the strawberries and cluster the remaining blueberries in the center. Spoon the remaining sauce artfully on top and garnish with the whole perfect strawberry and mint sprigs.

1 tablespoon freshly squeezed lemon
juice

1 pound seedless green grapes, stemmed
and halved lengthwise

1 pint fresh blueberries, stemmed

GARNISHES:

1 perfect large strawberry

3 sprigs mint, lemon verbena, or lemon
geranium

PER SERVING: 165–142 C   3–2 g P   2–1.8 g
TF   (0.5–0.4 g SAT)   36–31 g CARB   26–23
mg S   1.7–1.5 mg CH

POACHED SWEET RED CHERRIES WITH CRÈME FRAÎCHE

MAKES 4 SERVINGS

⅔ cup dry red wine
⅓ cup sugar
3 (3 × ½-inch) strips orange zest
1 vanilla bean, split lengthwise
6 peppercorns
1¼ pounds sweet dark red cherries,
halved and pitted
1 tablespoon kirsch
1 recipe Crème Fraîche (page 175)

PER SERVING: 219 C   5 g P   2 g TF   (0.9
g SAT)   45 g CARB   58 mg S   4 mg CH

Serve when cherries are at their peak of flavor. This recipe will be better if you prepare it one day and serve it the next.

Place the wine, sugar, orange zest, vanilla bean, and peppercorns in a medium-size heavy saucepan, set over moderate heat, and bring to a boil. Add the cherries, adjust the heat so that the wine mixture bubbles gently, cover, and simmer 10 minutes until the cherries are tender. Using a slotted spoon, lift the cherries to a heatproof serving bowl. Raise the heat under the wine mixture to high and boil, uncovered, 3 to 4 minutes until slightly thickened. Strain, mix in the kirsch, and pour over the cherries. Cover and chill several hours or overnight.

Prepare the Crème Fraîche as directed; chill until ready to serve. Just before serving, drift the cherries with some of the Crème Fraîche and pass the remainder.

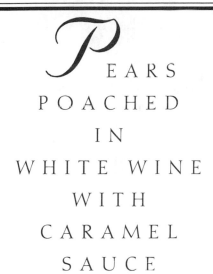

PEARS POACHED IN WHITE WINE WITH CARAMEL SAUCE

MAKES 4 SERVINGS

2 cups dry white wine
½ cup sugar
2 (3 × 1-inch) strips lemon zest
10 peppercorns
2 slices peeled fresh ginger, each about ¼ inch thick
1 vanilla bean, split lengthwise
4 large firm-ripe pears (Boscs or Bartletts are best), peeled and cored from the blossom end but left whole
1 recipe Caramel Sauce (page 183)

PER SERVING: 262 C   3 g P   3.6 g TF   (0.5 g SAT)   83 g CARB   40 mg S   1.3 mg CH

Use firm-ripe pears for this recipe and for a pretty presentation leave the stems intact.

Place the wine, sugar, lemon zest, peppercorns, ginger, and vanilla bean in a saucepan large enough to hold the pears in a single layer. Set over moderate heat and bring to a boil. Add the pears, standing them on their blossom ends. Adjust the heat so that the wine mixture bubbles gently, cover, and simmer 1 hour or until the pears are tender. Let the pears cool in the poaching mixture, then refrigerate in the mixture at least 4 hours.

When ready to serve, prepare the Caramel Sauce as directed. Pool a bit of the sauce on each of 4 dessert plates, stand a well-drained pear in the center of each, and serve.

$\mathcal{L}$ARANJAS À LISBONENSE (LISBON-STYLE ORANGES)

MAKES 8 SERVINGS

8 large navel oranges
1¾ cups sugar
⅞ cup cold water
1 (10-ounce) package unsweetened frozen raspberries, partially thawed, with their juice
½ cup red currant jelly
¼ cup Malmsey (sweet Madeira wine)
2 tablespoons Grand Marnier

PER SERVING: 234 C   2 g P   0.5 g TF
(0 g SAT)   56 g CARB   6 mg S   0 mg CH

$\mathcal{I}$t's odd that the Portuguese, who load their desserts with egg yolks and sugar, would come up with this zero-cholesterol classic. With its combination of scarlet and orange, it's as showy as it is delicious.

$\mathcal{U}$sing a swivel-bladed vegetable peeler, remove the zest from the oranges, cut it lengthwise into ⅛-inch-wide strips, and blanch 10 minutes in boiling water; drain and reserve. Boil the sugar and water 5 minutes in an uncovered medium-size heavy saucepan, add the orange zest, reduce the heat to low, and simmer, uncovered, 15 minutes. Drain and reserve.

$\mathcal{C}$ombine the raspberries, jelly, Malmsey, and Grand Marnier by buzzing in a food processor or electric blender at high speed 15 to 20 seconds; press through a fine sieve and set aside.

$\mathcal{P}$eel all rind and white pith from the oranges, then slice them crosswise ¼ inch thick. Layer the oranges and raspberry mixture into a 2-quart crystal bowl, beginning with the oranges and ending with the raspberry mixture. Pile the candied orange zest on top and serve.

2

PUDDINGS,

MOUSSES,

AND

SOUFFLÉS

COEUR
À LA CRÈME

MAKES 10 SERVINGS

CHEESE MIXTURE:

1 (1-pound) container lowfat
(1 percent) cottage cheese

1 (8-ounce) package neufschâtel
(light cream cheese)

⅓ cup sugar

½ teaspoon freshly squeezed lemon juice

SAUCE:

1 (10-ounce) package frozen unsweetened
raspberries or strawberries, thawed,
with their juice

3 tablespoons sugar

½ teaspoon freshly squeezed lemon juice

PER SERVING: 147 C   8 g P   6 g TF   (3.6 g
SAT)   16 g CARB   275 mg S   19 mg CH

ade the French way, coeur à la crème simply oozes butterfat. This one has had most of it removed, yet it's surprisingly creamy and rich.

*L*ine a *coeur à la crème* mold (a heart-shaped mold with drainage holes in the bottom) with a double thickness of dampened cheesecloth, allowing a 2-inch overhang.

For the Cheese Mixture: Combine the cottage cheese, neufschâtel, sugar, and lemon juice by churning about 2 minutes in a food processor until very smooth. Spoon into the prepared mold, place the mold upright on a plate, and refrigerate overnight.

For the Sauce: Purée the berries with the sugar and lemon juice by buzzing about 1 minute in a food processor; if using raspberries, also push through a fine sieve. Refrigerate until ready to serve.

To serve, invert the mold on a serving plate with the cheesecloth overhang in your hands. Carefully lift off the mold, then gently remove the cheesecloth. Pour some of the sauce over the Coeur à la Crème and pass the rest.

PASHKA

MAKES 10 TO 12 SERVINGS

3 envelopes unflavored gelatin
1 cup evaporated skim milk
⅔ cup sugar
4 teaspoons butter flavor granules
2 (1-pound) containers lowfat (1 percent)
no-salt-added cottage cheese
1 cup Labna (page 176)
1 cup diced mixed candied fruits
½ cup finely chopped blanched almonds
2 teaspoons vanilla

PER SERVING: 305–254 C   23–19 g P
4.5–3.6 g TF   (0.6–0.5 g SAT)   43–35 g
CARB   204–170 mg S   7.7–6.4 mg CH

The classic Russian Easter dessert stripped of most of its cholesterol. The authentic version doesn't stint on butter, heavy cream, or egg yolks.

Sprinkle the gelatin over the bottom of a small saucepan, pour in the milk, and let stand for 10 minutes. Set over moderately low heat and cook, stirring often, for 12 to 15 minutes until the gelatin dissolves completely. Mix in the sugar and butter granules and stir until dissolved; set aside. Purée the cheese until absolutely smooth by churning in a food processor or electric blender at high speed 1 minute. Add the Labna and pulse quickly to incorporate. Transfer to a large bowl, then fold in the gelatin mixture and all remaining ingredients. Pour into a tall 2-quart mold (plain or fluted), cover with a plate, and refrigerate for 8 hours or overnight until set. To unmold, dip the mold briefly in hot water, loosen the Pashka around the edge with a small spatula, then invert on a plate. Cut into slim wedges and serve.

CHOCOLATE CHESTNUT MOLD

MAKES 6 SERVINGS

⅓ cup unsweetened Dutch process cocoa
powder

2½ tablespoons evaporated skim milk

1 (15½-ounce) can chestnuts in water,
well drained

¾ cup sugar

2 tablespoons unsalted soft tub margarine (not extra-light)

1½ tablespoons dark rum or coffee
liqueur

½ teaspoon vanilla

OPTIONAL GARNISHES:

1 cup Mock Whipped Cream (page 174)
Candied violets or roses

PER SERVING: 220 C   2 g P   5 g TF   (1 g
SAT)   42 g CARB   56 mg S   0.3 mg CH

Line a 2½- to 3-cup bowl with plastic food wrap, smoothing it all around and leaving an overhang of about 2 inches. Blend the cocoa and milk and set aside. Combine the chestnuts and sugar by churning in a food processor 20 seconds; add the margarine and churn 15 to 20 seconds until absolutely smooth. Add the rum, vanilla, and cocoa mixture and pulse to combine. Spoon into the lined bowl, cover, and refrigerate overnight.

To serve, invert the mold onto a serving plate, carefully lift off the bowl, and remove the plastic wrap. Cut into wedges and serve or, if you like, garnish first: spoon Mock Whipped Cream into a pastry bag fitted with a medium star tip and pipe a starburst design over the top and down the sides of the mold. Sprig with candied violets, cut into 6 wedges, and serve.

RUTH'S CHOCOLATE BREAD PUDDING

MAKES 6 SERVINGS

¼ cup unsweetened Dutch process
cocoa powder

¾ cup sugar

1½ cups evaporated skim milk

½ cup whole milk

1½ tablespoons extra-light olive oil, walnut or hazelnut oil

1 cup very firmly packed soft bread
crumbs (not too fine; you'll need about
6 slices firm-textured white bread)

½ cup liquid egg substitute

1 teaspoon vanilla

¼ teaspoon ground cinnamon

TOPPING:

Crème Anglaise (page 178) or
Mock Whipped Cream (page 174)

PER SERVING (IF TOPPED WITH CRÈME
ANGLAISE): 284 C   11 g P   6.8 g TF   (2.2 g
SAT)   47 g CARB   209 mg S   10.7 mg CH

PER SERVING (IF TOPPED WITH MOCK
WHIPPED CREAM): 242 C   9 g P
5.3 g TF   (1.4 g SAT)   41 g CARB
185 mg S   6 mg CH

A friend and fellow chocoholic who has been put on a low-cholesterol diet told me that one of her favorite desserts is the chocolate bread pudding her mother made when she was a child. But it, alas, is filled with high-cholesterol eggs and high-fat squares of chocolate. This slimmed-down version is as dense, dark, and delicious as the original, and she can enjoy it with impunity.

Combine the cocoa and sugar in a medium-size heavy saucepan, pressing out all lumps, then blend in the evaporated milk and whole milk. Set over moderately high heat and cook and stir 2 to 3 minutes until the sugar dissolves completely. Set off the heat, mix in the oil and bread crumbs, cover, and let stand at room temperature 1 hour.

Preheat the oven to moderate (350° F.). Stir the egg substitute, vanilla, and cinnamon into the chocolate mixture, and pour into a 6-cup soufflé dish that has been sprayed with nonstick vege- table cooking spray (preferably a butter-flavored one). Set in a large baking pan and pour enough hot water into the pan to come halfway up the sides of the soufflé dish.

Bake the pudding, uncovered, in the water bath in the preheated oven for 1 hour or until set like custard. Remove from the oven and from the water bath and cool 30 minutes. Serve warm, topped by a couple of tablespoons of either Crème Anglaise or Mock Whipped Cream.

STEAMED CHOCOLATE HAZELNUT PUDDING

MAKES 6 SERVINGS

2 cups sifted all-purpose flour
¾ cup firmly packed light brown sugar
3 tablespoons unsweetened Dutch process cocoa powder
1 teaspoon baking soda
1 cup lowfat buttermilk
3½ tablespoons hazelnut or walnut oil blended with 1 tablespoon butter flavor granules
1 teaspoon vanilla

OPTIONAL TOPPING:

Mock Whipped Cream (page 174)

PER SERVING: 343 C   6 g P   9.3 g TF   (1 g SAT)   60 g CARB   296 mg S   2 mg CH

Few of us bother to make steamed puddings these days and that's a shame. They are a good choice for cholesterol-counters because they contain no eggs at all and also because poly- or monounsaturated oils can be substituted successfully for the butter. In this recipe, for example, I've used hazelnut oil. One word of caution: make sure the hazelnut oil you use is absolutely fresh and sweet-smelling. Rancid oil will ruin the pudding.

Oil a 6- to 8-cup steamed pudding mold well with vegetable oil, paying particular attention to the fluting and central tube; don't forget to oil the lid, too. Set the mold aside. Set a large deep kettle containing 1 inch of water over moderate heat, cover, and bring to a boil.

Meanwhile, pulse the flour, sugar, cocoa, and soda 4 to 6 times in a food processor fitted with the metal chopping blade until uniformly fine. Transfer to a large mixing bowl and make a well in the center. In a 1-pint measuring cup, whisk the buttermilk with the oil mixture and vanilla until uniformly creamy. Dump into the well in the dry ingredients and stir just to mix. The batter will be lumpy but do not stir further or the pudding will be tough.

Spoon the batter into the prepared mold and snap on the lid. Place a rack in the kettle with the boiling water, then stand the mold on the rack, making sure that the bottom of the mold doesn't touch the water. Adjust the heat so that the water in the kettle bubbles very gently, cover the kettle, and steam the pudding for 1 hour and 10 minutes. If at any point the kettle threatens to boil dry, add a little additional boiling water, again making certain that it does not touch the bottom of the pudding mold.

$\mathcal{L}$ift the pudding mold from the kettle, stand upright on a wire rack, and let the pudding cool, still covered, for 15 minutes. Uncover the mold and very carefully loosen the pudding around the edges and around the central tube with a thin-bladed knife. Invert the pudding on a serving plate and serve warm, accompanied, if you like, with Mock Whipped Cream.

GLORIOUS, GUILT-FREE CHOCOLATE MOUSSE

MAKES 6 TO 8 SERVINGS

3½ teaspoons unflavored gelatin

⅓ cup unsweetened Dutch process cocoa powder

⅛ teaspoon freshly ground black pepper

⅛ teaspoon ground cinnamon

1 cup evaporated skim milk

2 tablespoons unsalted soft tub margarine (not extra-light)

⅓ cup liquid egg substitute

2 teaspoons vanilla

⅓ cup sugar

½ cup boiling water

6 tablespoons meringue powder (see page xviii)

OPTIONAL GARNISHES:

Mock Whipped Cream (page 174)
Candied violets

PER SERVING: 166–125 C   8–6 g P
4.6–3.5 g TF   (1.2–0.9 g SAT)   25–18 g
CARB   128–96 mg S   1.7–1.3 mg CH

And do try the easy Orange-Mocha variation, which follows.

Combine the gelatin, cocoa, pepper, and cinnamon in a small heavy saucepan, pressing out all lumps; mix in the milk, and let stand 10 minutes at room temperature. Set over moderate heat and cook and stir 3 minutes until the gelatin dissolves completely. Drop in the margarine and stir until it melts. Now blend a little of the hot mixture into the egg substitute, stir back into the pan, reduce the heat to moderately low, and heat, whisking hard, 2 minutes until very thick. Transfer to a large heatproof bowl, mix in the vanilla, and set in an ice bath. Chill, whisking often, 15 to 20 minutes until very thick and almost set.

Combine the sugar and boiling water in the large bowl of an electric mixer (preferably one with a wire whip attachment), add the meringue powder, and beat at highest mixer speed 3 minutes until the consistency of 7-minute icing. Whisk about 1 cup of the meringue into the chocolate mixture to lighten it—you may have to beat very hard to incorporate it smoothly. Then whisk in ½ the remaining meringue. Finally, fold in the remaining meringue gently but thoroughly until no streaks of white or brown show. Cover and refrigerate 1 to 2 hours until set.

Spoon the mousse into stemmed goblets and if you like, drift, with Mock Whipped Cream and sprig with candied violets. Or, if you prefer, layer the mousse and "whipped cream" into parfait glasses.

VARIATION :

 Orange-Mocha Mousse (*6 to 8 servings*): Prepare as directed above but omit the cinnamon; add 1½ teaspoons instant espresso coffee crystals and 1 teaspoon finely grated orange zest, and heat along with the gelatin mixture. Also mix in 2 tablespoons coffee liqueur along with the vanilla. When serving, top, if you like, with dollops of Mock Whipped Cream and sprinklings of finely julienned orange zest.

PER SERVING: 181–136 C   8–6 g P   4.6–3.5 g TF   (1.2–0.9 g SAT)   26–20 g CARB   128–96 mg S   1.7–1.3 mg CH

DOUBLE CHOCOLATE POTS DE CRÈME

MAKES 6 SERVINGS

2 cups whole milk

¼ cup unsweetened Dutch process cocoa powder

¾ cup sugar

1 (7.5 ounce) container liquid egg substitute

1½ teaspoons vanilla

Pinch of salt

1 ounce semisweet chocolate, coarsely chopped

PER SERVING: 199 C   7 g P   5 g TF   (3 g SAT)   34 g CARB   139 mg S   11.4 mg CH

*A*dding 1 ounce of semisweet chocolate increases the saturated fats in this recipe only slightly but enriches the flavor no end.

*P*reheat the oven to moderate (350° F.). Blend ½ cup of the milk with the cocoa in a medium-size bowl, then whisk in the sugar, egg substitute, vanilla, and salt and set aside. Heat the remaining milk and the chocolate in a small heavy saucepan over low heat 3 to 4 minutes, stirring occasionally, until the chocolate melts. Cool 5 minutes, then whisk into the cocoa mixture. Pour into 6 (6-ounce) ramekins. Place in a pan large enough to hold all the ramekins without crowding and cover each with foil. Set the pan in the lower third of the oven and pour in enough hot water to come halfway up the sides of the ramekins.

*B*ake the *pots de crème* in the preheated oven about 45 minutes or until set like custard. Remove from the oven and from the water bath, cool to room temperature, then refrigerate, still covered, and serve cold.

Strawberry Shortcake *(page 12)*

CLOCKWISE FROM TOP RIGHT:
LEMON ANGEL PIE *(page 88)*,
CANNOLI *(page 96)*,
LITTLE LINZERS *(page 80)*,
STAR-SPANGLED CRANBERRY-
APPLE TART *(page 79)*

STRAWBERRY SORBET WITH
FRESH STRAWBERRY COULIS
(page 171)

Mocha
POTS
DE CRÈME

MAKES 6 SERVINGS

1 cup whole milk
1 cup lowfat (1 percent) milk
3 tablespoons ground coffee (not instant)
¼ cup unsweetened Dutch process
cocoa powder
½ cup granulated sugar
¼ cup firmly packed light brown sugar
1 (7.5-ounce) container liquid
egg substitute
2 teaspoons coffee liqueur or dark rum
Pinch of salt

PER SERVING: 171 C   7 g P   2.5 g TF
(1.5 g SAT)   32 g CARB   144 mg S
7.3 mg CH

𝒫reheat the oven to moderate (350° F.). In a small heavy saucepan set over moderate heat, bring the whole milk, ½ cup of the lowfat milk, and the coffee to a simmer; remove from the heat, cover, and steep 10 minutes. Strain through a coffee filter and reserve. Blend the cocoa and the remaining lowfat milk, then gently whisk in (so you don't create bubbles) the coffee mixture, granulated and brown sugars, the egg substitute, coffee liqueur, and salt. Pour into 6 (6-ounce) ramekins. Place in a pan large enough to hold all the ramekins without crowding and cover each with foil. Set the pan in the lower third of the oven and pour in enough hot water to come halfway up the sides of the ramekins.

𝐵ake the *pots de crème* in the preheated oven about 45 minutes or until set like custard. Remove from the oven and from the water bath, cool to room temperature, then refrigerate, still covered, and serve cold.

$\mathcal{V}$ANILLA POTS DE CRÈME

MAKES 6 SERVINGS

2 cups whole milk
1 vanilla bean, split lengthwise
½ cup sugar
Pinch of salt
1 cup liquid egg substitute

PER SERVING: 133 C   6 g P   2.7 g TF   (1.7 g SAT)   21 g CARB   115 mg S   11.4 mg CH

This is old-fashioned baked custard—French-style. Its intense vanilla flavoring comes from a vanilla bean, not from an extract. And it is not dusted with freshly grated nutmeg, which is the American way.

$\mathcal{P}$reheat the oven to moderate (350° F.). Place the milk, vanilla bean, ¼ cup of the sugar, and the salt in a medium-size heavy saucepan, set over low heat, and bring to a simmer; remove from the heat, cover, and steep 20 minutes. Lightly whisk together the remaining sugar and the egg substitute (avoid creating bubbles). Scrape the seeds from the vanilla bean into the milk (discard the pod), then whisk gently into the egg substitute mixture. Pour into 6 (6-ounce) ramekins. Place in a pan large enough to hold all the ramekins without crowding and cover each with foil. Set the pan in the lower third of the oven and pour in enough hot water to come halfway up the sides of the ramekins.

$\mathcal{B}$ake the *pots de crème* in the preheated oven about 45 minutes or until set like custard. Remove from the oven and from the water bath, cool to room temperature, then refrigerate, still covered, and serve cold.

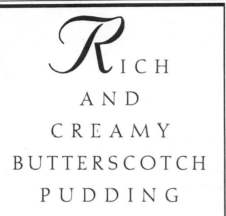

RICH AND CREAMY BUTTERSCOTCH PUDDING

MAKES 4 SERVINGS

½ cup firmly packed dark brown sugar
¼ cup cornstarch
Pinch of salt
2 cups whole milk
2 egg whites
¾ teaspoon vanilla
2 tablespoons unsalted soft tub margarine (not extra-light)

PER SERVING: 269 C   6 g P   9.6 g TF
(3.5 g SAT)   40 g CARB   129 mg S
17 mg CH

*B*lend ¼ cup of the brown sugar, the cornstarch, and salt in a medium-size bowl. Whisk in ¼ cup of the milk, then the egg whites. Heat the remaining milk and sugar in a medium-size heavy saucepan over low heat just until boiling. Blend a little of the hot milk mixture into the cornstarch mixture, then stir all into the pan and cook, stirring constantly, over moderately low heat just until the mixture boils. Boil 2 minutes, whisking all the while, until thick. Strain, stir in the vanilla and margarine, and cool to room temperature, stirring occasionally to prevent a "skin" from forming on the surface of the pudding. Spoon into individual dessert goblets and chill well before serving.

ÎLE
FLOTANTE

MAKES 8 SERVINGS

CARAMEL:

½ cup sugar

⅓ cup water

1½ teaspoons freshly squeezed
lemon juice

MERINGUES:

4 egg whites, at room temperature

Pinch of salt

Pinch of cream of tartar

½ cup sugar

1 teaspoon vanilla

RASPBERRY SAUCE:

3 cups frozen unsweetened raspberries,
thawed, with their juice

6 tablespoons sugar

2½ tablespoons framboise (raspberry
liqueur)

PER SERVING: 181 C   2 g P   0.5 g TF   (0 g
SAT)   42 g CARB   44 mg S   0 mg CH

The classic floating island pudding consists of caramelized poached meringues scudding across a lake of custard. This low-cholesterol version substitutes raspberry sauce for custard and is more beautiful, flavorful, and healthful.

For the Caramel: Combine the sugar, water, and lemon juice in a small heavy saucepan, set over moderately high heat, and cook, uncovered, without stirring until the mixture turns amber, about 4 minutes. Pour the caramel into 8 (8-ounce) oven-proof ramekins or molds, tipping them to coat the bottoms.

For the Meringues: Preheat the oven to moderate (350° F.). Beat the egg whites and salt in the large bowl of an electric mixer at high speed until frothy, add the cream of tartar, and continue beating until soft peaks begin to form. Gradually add the sugar, beating all the while, until the mixture is stiff and glossy; beat in the vanilla. Spoon the meringue into the prepared molds and place in a baking pan large enough to hold them in a single layer without touching one another. Pour enough hot water into the pan to come halfway up the sides of the molds. Bake, uncovered, in the preheated oven 15 minutes or until set. Remove the molds from the oven and from the water bath and cool upright on a wire rack. Refrigerate until ready to serve.

For the Raspberry Sauce: Purée the berries with the sugar and framboise by buzzing about 1 minute in a food processor; force through a fine sieve and refrigerate until ready to serve.

To serve, ladle some of the sauce onto each of 8 dessert plates, then invert a meringue on top of each, letting it ease out of the mold.

ALGARVE POACHED MERINGUE RING WITH FRESH STRAWBERRIES

MAKES 8 SERVINGS

MERINGUE:

6 extra-large egg whites
¼ teaspoon cream of tartar
½ cup granulated sugar
½ cup superfine sugar
1½ teaspoons freshly squeezed
lemon juice
¾ teaspoon vanilla
½ teaspoon almond extract

TOPPING:

1 pint fresh strawberries, hulled and
sliced thin
¼ cup superfine sugar
1 tablespoon freshly squeezed
lemon juice
2 tablespoons Cointreau

PER SERVING: 160 C   3 g P   0.1 g TF
(0 g SAT)   36 g CARB   47 mg S   0 mg CH

On my first trip to Portugal's Algarve Province nearly 30 years ago, I ordered a funny-sounding dessert in a little waterfront restaurant. It turned out to be a snowy poached meringue sloshed with apricot sauce. I couldn't wait to get back home and work out the recipe. Today I more often serve the meringue with sliced strawberries, but if you'd like to try the original apricot version, substitute *Faro Apricot Sauce (page 187)* for the topping given below.

For the Meringue: Preheat the oven to moderately slow (325° F.). Beat the egg whites and cream of tartar until frothy at moderately slow mixer speed. Add the granulated sugar, then the superfine sugar, in each instance 1 tablespoon at a time, beating well after each addition. Raise the mixer speed to high, sprinkle the lemon juice, vanilla, and almond extract over the meringue, and beat 2 to 3 minutes until the mixture peaks stiffly. Pack into an ungreased 6-cup ring mold, set in a large shallow baking pan, and pour in enough cold water to come halfway up the sides of the mold.

Bake, uncovered, in the water bath in the preheated oven, about 1 hour until the meringue is puffed, pale tan, and begins to pull from the sides of the mold. Remove the meringue from the oven and from the water bath, set upright on a wire rack, and cool to room temperature.

Meanwhile, Prepare the Topping: Place all ingredients in a large nonmetallic bowl, toss lightly, cover, and let stand at room temperature until ready to serve.

To Serve: Using a small thin-bladed spatula, carefully loosen the meringue around the edge and around the central tube, then invert onto a large round platter. Fill the central well of the meringue with strawberries and wreathe the balance around the base.

$\mathcal{P}$ UDIM
MOLOTOV

MAKES 8 SERVINGS

FOR PREPARING THE PAN:

1 tablespoon unsalted soft tub margarine
(not extra-light)

3 tablespoons granulated sugar

PUDDING:

1 cup granulated sugar

1½ cups boiling water

2 tablespoons freshly squeezed
lemon juice

1½ cups egg whites (about 9 jumbo or
extra-large eggs)

2 teaspoons vanilla

1 cup sifted confectioners' sugar

PER SERVING: 203 C   5 g P   1.4 g TF   (0.2
g SAT)   43 g CARB   79 mg S   0 mg CH

You could best describe this popular Portuguese dessert as a burnt-sugar meringue topped with burnt-sugar syrup. No one knows the origin of the pudding (or its unlikely name) and this particular recipe is just one of many variations on the theme. Most Portuguese egg sweets are made with yolks only, and it's just possible that some thrifty cook (could her name possibly have been Molotov?) invented this cloud-light dessert because she was tired of pitching out the whites. It's delicious warm or at room temperature.

$\mathcal{G}$rease the bottom, sides, and central tube of a 10-inch tube pan smoothly with the margarine, add the sugar, then tilt the pan from side to side until all surfaces are evenly coated with sugar. Tap out the excess sugar and set the pan aside.

For the Pudding: Place the granulated sugar in a medium-size deep heavy skillet; set, uncovered, over moderately low heat, and let the sugar melt. This will take about 30 minutes. Do not stir the sugar as it melts—you'll wind up with hard lumps that are difficult to dissolve. But do shake the pan from time to time so that the sugar liquefies evenly and turns a rich amber brown. (If the sugar threatens to blacken, reduce the heat to low.) Add the water slowly—stand back, it will sputter wildly—then pour in the lemon juice, reduce the heat to low, and simmer, uncovered, without stirring, for about 30 minutes or until all the burnt sugar has dissolved and the mixture is about the consistency of pancake syrup. Turn the heat to its lowest point, cover the syrup, and keep warm.

$\mathcal{P}$reheat the oven to moderate (350° F.). Beat the egg whites and vanilla at highest mixer speed until frothy, then drizzle in ½ cup of burnt sugar syrup in the finest of streams, beating all the while (keep the remaining syrup warm in the covered pan at the back of the stove). Reduce the mixer speed to moderate and beat in 4 tablespoons of the confectioners' sugar, 1 tablespoon at a time. The beaten whites should not peak—even softly—but billow and flow when the bowl is tilted. Sift the remaining confectioners' sugar over the beaten whites and fold in gently but thoroughly.

Pour the pudding batter into the prepared pan, smoothing the top, then set in a large roasting pan and pour about 1 inch of hot water into the roasting pan to form a water bath. Bake the pudding, uncovered, in the water bath on the middle shelf of the preheated oven for about 45 minutes or until puffed and nicely browned—the pudding should quiver ever so slightly when you nudge the pan. Remove from the oven and from the water bath.

Quickly spray 2 (12-inch) squares of heavy-duty aluminum foil with nonstick vegetable cooking spray. Carefully loosen the pudding around the edges and around the central tube with a thin-bladed spatula that has been sprayed with non-stick vegetable cooking spray. Place one of the foil squares, sprayed-side-down, on top of the pudding pan, invert the pudding, and lift off the pan. Now quickly lay the second square of foil, sprayed-side-down, on top of the pudding, invert once again so that the pudding is right-side-up, and ease onto a large round platter, foil and all. With scissors, snip away all the foil that shows.

Drizzle the reserved warm burnt sugar syrup artfully over the Pudim Molotov, cut into large wedges, and serve.

ORANGE SOUFFLÉ

MAKES 4 TO 6 SERVINGS

FOR PREPARING THE
SOUFFLÉ DISH:

Nonstick vegetable cooking spray
2 tablespoons granulated sugar

SOUFFLÉ:

2 tablespoons unsalted soft tub
   margarine (not extra-light)
¾ cup evaporated skim milk
2 tablespoons all-purpose flour
½ cup granulated sugar
¾ cup liquid egg substitute
2 tablespoons finely grated orange zest
2 tablespoons Grand Marnier
4 extra-large egg whites
¼ teaspoon cream of tartar
⅛ teaspoon salt
4 tablespoons confectioners' sugar

PER SERVING: 291–194 C   12–8 g P
5.8–3.9 g TF (1.0–0.7 g SAT)   47–31 g
CARB   247–165 mg S   1.9–1.3 mg CH

*W*here most people go wrong in making soufflés is in overbeating the egg whites. They should just billow and peak softly, not stand in stiff points when the beater is withdrawn.

*S*et a heavy baking sheet on the middle oven shelf and preheat the oven to hot (400° F.). Lightly spray a 1½-quart soufflé dish with the cooking spray, add the 2 tablespoons sugar, and tilt the dish to one side, then another, until evenly coated with sugar. Rap the dish lightly and tap out the excess sugar, then set the dish aside.

For the Soufflé: Bring the margarine and milk to a simmer in a medium-size heavy saucepan over moderately low heat. Meanwhile, combine the flour and granulated sugar in a medium-size heatproof mixing bowl; blend in the egg substitute. Slowly pour in the hot milk mixture, whisking all the while, then stir back into the saucepan. Set over moderately low heat and cook, whisking vigorously, 3 to 5 minutes until very thick. Press at once through a fine sieve set over a large heatproof bowl, then set this bowl in an ice bath and cool the thickened sauce 15 minutes, stirring occasionally. Mix in the orange zest and Grand Marnier.

*B*eat the egg whites with the cream of tartar and salt until frothy at moderate electric mixer speed, then, beating all the while, add the confectioners' sugar, 1 tablespoon at a time. Stop beating as soon as the whites peak softly. Mix about 1 cup of the beaten whites into the thickened sauce, then add the remaining beaten whites and fold in gently but thoroughly until no streaks of white or yellow remain.

*P*our the soufflé batter into the prepared dish, set on the hot baking sheet in the preheated oven, reduce the oven temperature at once to moderately hot (375° F.), and bake 25 to 30 minutes until the soufflé is puffed, browned, and quivers slightly when you nudge the dish. Rush the soufflé to the table and serve.

FRESH GINGER SOUFFLÉ

MAKES 6 SERVINGS

FOR PREPARING THE SOUFFLÉ DISH:

Nonstick vegetable cooking spray
2 tablespoons sugar

SOUFFLÉ:

1 piece fresh ginger, 3 inches long, peeled and thinly sliced (a generous ½ cup)

1¼ cups lowfat (1 percent) milk

4½ tablespoons sugar

6 (2½ × ½-inch) strips lime zest

2 tablespoons all-purpose flour

2 tablespoons unsalted soft tub margarine (not extra-light)

⅔ cup liquid egg substitute

2½ tablespoons chopped crystallized ginger

5 egg whites

⅛ teaspoon salt

⅛ teaspoon cream of tartar

PER SERVING: 172 C   7 g P   4.4 g TF   (1 g SAT)   26 g CARB   158 mg S   2 mg CH

Blanching fresh ginger for 30 seconds makes it release more flavor.

Lightly spray a 1½-quart soufflé dish with the cooking spray, add the 2 tablespoons sugar, and tilt the dish to one side, then another, until evenly coated with sugar, and reserve. Rap the dish lightly, tap out and reserve the excess sugar. Make a 3-inch-wide band of aluminum foil long enough to wrap around the soufflé dish, spray with nonstick vegetable cooking spray, and dust with the reserved sugar. Wrap the band around the top of the soufflé dish, sugared-side-in, and secure with cellophane tape. Set the dish aside.

For the Soufflé: Blanch the fresh ginger for 30 seconds in boiling water and drain well. Place the milk, blanched ginger, 2½ tablespoons of the sugar, and the lime zest in a medium-size heavy saucepan, set over moderately low heat, and heat just until small bubbles appear around the edge of the pan. Remove from the heat, cover, and let stand at room temperature 1 hour.

Set a heavy baking sheet on a shelf positioned in the lower third of the oven and preheat the oven to moderately hot (375° F.). Strain the milk mixture through a fine sieve, pushing down to extract as much liquid as possible. Place the flour in a medium-size heavy saucepan and gradually whisk in the milk mixture. Set over moderately low heat and cook, stirring constantly, 3 minutes until thickened. Off the heat, whisk in the margarine, then the egg substitute; continue whisking until well combined. Mix in the crystallized ginger.

Beat the egg whites with the salt in the large bowl of an electric mixer (preferably one with a wire whip attachment) until frothy. Add the cream of tartar and beat to soft peaks. Gradually beat in the remaining 2 tablespoons sugar—the beaten whites should be moist and billowing. Stir about 1 cup of the beaten whites into the milk mixture to lighten it, then gently fold in the remaining whites.

*P*our into the prepared soufflé dish, set on the baking sheet, and bake about 25 minutes in the preheated oven until the soufflé is puffed, browned, and quivers slightly when you nudge the dish. Carefully remove the foil collar, rush the soufflé to the table, and serve.

THE SOUFFLÉ FOR CHOCOHOLICS

MAKES 6 SERVINGS

FOR PREPARING THE SOUFFLÉ DISH:

Nonstick vegetable cooking spray

2 tablespoons granulated sugar

SOUFFLÉ:

½ cup unsweetened Dutch process cocoa powder

2 tablespoons firmly packed dark brown sugar

¼ cup hot water

2 tablespoons all-purpose flour

4 tablespoons granulated sugar

1 cup evaporated skim milk

1 tablespoon butter flavor granules

2 tablespoons extra-light olive oil or vegetable oil (canola, safflower, sunflower, corn oil, etc.)

⅔ cup liquid egg substitute

1 teaspoon vanilla

4 extra-large egg whites

⅛ teaspoon salt

⅛ teaspoon cream of tartar

Set a heavy baking sheet on a shelf positioned in the lower third of the oven and preheat the oven to moderately hot (375° F.). Lightly spray a 1½-quart soufflé dish with the cooking spray, add the 2 tablespoons sugar, and tilt the dish to one side, then another, until evenly coated with sugar. Rap the dish lightly, tap out and reserve the excess sugar. Make a 3-inch-wide band of aluminum foil long enough to wrap around the soufflé dish, spray with nonstick vegetable cooking spray, and dust with the reserved sugar. Wrap the band around the top of the soufflé dish, sugared side in, and secure with cellophane tape. Set the dish aside.

For the Soufflé: Combine the cocoa, brown sugar, and water in a small bowl, stirring until smooth; set aside. Whisk together the flour, 2 tablespoons of the granulated sugar, and the milk in a medium-size heavy saucepan, set over moderately low heat, and cook, stirring constantly, 3 minutes until thickened and smooth. Blend in the cocoa mixture. Remove from the heat and, whisking all the while, beat in the butter granules, then the oil, egg substitute, and vanilla. Continue whisking until smooth and transfer to a large bowl.

Beat the egg whites with the salt in the large bowl of an electric mixer (preferably one with a wire whip attachment) until frothy. Add the cream of tartar and beat to soft peaks. Gradually beat in the remaining 2 tablespoons granulated sugar—the beaten whites should be moist and billowing. Stir about 1 cup of the beaten whites into the cocoa mixture to lighten it, then gently fold in the remaining whites until no streaks of brown or white remain (the soufflé batter will be quite thin).

Pour into the prepared soufflé dish, set on the baking sheet, and bake about 35 minutes in the preheated oven until the soufflé is puffed, browned, and quivers slightly when you nudge

OPTIONAL TOPPING:

1 teaspoon confectioners' sugar

PER SERVING: 200 C   10 g P
6.3. g TF   (1.5 g SAT)   29 g CARB
310 mg S   2 mg CH

the dish. Very carefully remove the foil collar, dust, if you like, with the confectioners' sugar, then rush the soufflé to the table, and serve.

V A R I A T I O N :

♣ *Mocha Soufflé (6 servings):* Prepare as directed, but mix 1 tablespoon instant espresso coffee crystals with the cocoa at the outset and increase the amount of water to ⅓ cup.

PER SERVING: 200 C   10 g P   6.3 g TF   (1.5 g SAT)   29 g CARB   310 mg S   2 mg CH

Riz

À

L'IMPÉRATRICE

MAKES 14 SERVINGS

6½ cups cold water

1½ cups long-grain white rice

3¾ cups whole milk

3½ teaspoons unflavored gelatin

1½ cups finely diced mixed candied
fruits

3 tablespoons Grand Marnier or
Cointreau

¼ cup evaporated skim mlk

1 cup sugar

2 vanilla beans, split lengthwise

2 tablespoons unsalted soft tub
margarine (not extra-light)

½ cup liquid egg substitute

Finely grated zest of 2 large oranges

¾ cup Labna (page 176) or lowfat (1
percent) cottage cheese puréed until
absolutely smooth

This low-fat, low-cholesterol dessert seems almost as rich as the diet-busting original. And it's every bit as glamorous. Tip: if you have a food processor—or even a mini electric food chopper—here's a quick way to grate the orange zest. Using a vegetable peeler, remove the zest (colored part of the rind) from the oranges in long thin strips and add to the food processor along with ½ cup of the sugar. Churn for about a minute until uniformly fine, then mix into the hot custard after the gelatin has dissolved. *You should prepare this dessert well ahead of time because it must chill at least 8 hours before it's served.*

*B*ring 6 cups of the water to a boil in a large heavy saucepan over moderate heat, stir in the rice, and as soon as the water returns to a rolling boil, drain the rice. Return to the pan, add 2 cups of the whole milk, bring to a simmer, then turn the heat to very low, cover, and cook for 30 minutes or until the rice is fluffy-tender and all the milk has been absorbed.

*M*eanwhile, put the gelatin to soak in the remaining ½ cup water and the candied fruits to macerate in the Grand Marnier. Next, bring the remaining 1¾ cups whole milk, the skim milk, sugar, vanilla beans, and margarine to a simmer in a small heavy saucepan over moderate heat. Whisk a bit of the hot milk mixture into the egg substitute, stir back into the pan, and cook and stir over moderately low heat until the custard thickens enough to coat a metal spoon. This may take as long as 20 minutes, so have patience. If you try to hurry things along by raising the heat, you risk curdling the custard. As soon as the sauce has thickened, remove from the heat and strain through a fine sieve. Scrape the tiny black seeds inside the vanilla beans into the custard and mix well; discard the beans. Add the softened gelatin to the hot custard and stir until the gelatin dissolves completely.

TOPPINGS AND GARNISHES:

1 cup sieved red raspberry or red currant
jam thinned with 1 tablespoon Grand
Marnier or Cointreau

Mock Whipped Cream (page 174) or
Vanilla Labna (page 177)

15 candied red cherries

8 candied green cherries, cut into leaf
shapes, or 1 (2-inch) piece angelica,
cut into leaf shapes

½ teaspoon each coarsely chopped
candied red and green cherries, tossed
together

PER SERVING: 402 C   7 g P   4 g TF   (1.7 g
SAT)   83 g CARB   156 mg S   9.7 mg CH

*M*ix the orange zest and Labna into the custard, then the candied fruits and any Grand Marnier remaining in the bottom of the bowl. Fluff the rice well with a fork and fold into the custard mixture. Pour into a fluted 2-quart mold and refrigerate for 8 hours or overnight.

To serve: Dip the mold briefly in hot water, loosen the Riz à l'Impératrice around the edge with a small spatula, then invert on a round plate or cake stand. Ladle the jam mixture over the top of the dessert, letting it run down the fluted sides. Pipe several rosettes or mound several poufs of Mock Whipped Cream on top. Pipe or spoon 15 little rosettes or poufs of Mock Whipped Cream around the base of the dessert, spacing evenly, then decorate each with a candied red cherry and sprig with a leaf or two cut from the candied green cherries. Finally, sprinkle the chopped candied cherries on top of the *Riz à l'Impératrice.* Cut into slim wedges and serve.

$\mathscr{H}$UNGARIAN
N O O D L E
P U D D I N G

MAKES 8 TO 10 SERVINGS

1 (12-ounce) package medium-wide
cholesterol-free noodles

¼ cup liquid egg substitute

⅔ cup granulated sugar

1 cup Labna (page 176) or lowfat
(1 percent) cottage cheese, puréed
until smooth

2 tablespoons unsalted soft tub
margarine (not extra-light)

3 teaspoons finely grated lemon zest

2 teaspoons vanilla

⅔ cup golden seedless raisins (sultanas)

3 extra-large egg whites

TOPPING:

1 tablespoon confectioners' sugar
(for dusting)

PER SERVING: 316–253 C   11–9 g P
3–2.4 g TF   (0.5–0.4 g SAT)   61–49 g
CARB   75–60 mg S   0–0 mg CH

$\mathcal{T}$hanks to the cholesterol-free noodles (sometimes called egg noodle substitute), now available in nearly every supermarket, this unusual pudding-torte is no longer off-limits to dieters. It's aromatic of lemon and vanilla but not very sweet. Serve as is or to be wholly unorthodox (and Americans will probably like it better this way), top with Crème Anglaise (page 178), Vanilla Labna (page 177), or Faro Apricot Sauce (page 187).

$\mathcal{P}$reheat the oven to moderate (350° F.). Spray the bottom and sides of a 4-quart soufflé dish well with nonstick vegetable cooking spray and set aside. Cook the noodles according to package directions.

$\mathcal{M}$eanwhile, place the egg substitute, granulated sugar, Labna, margarine, lemon zest, and vanilla in the small bowl of an electric mixer and beat at high speed for 2 to 3 minutes until quite thick; set aside. Place the raisins in a large heatproof bowl. As soon as the noodles are done, drain well and dump into the bowl with the raisins. Toss lightly, then add the sugar mixture, and stir well to mix. Beat the egg whites until stiff but not dry. Fold about 1 cup of the beaten whites into the noodle mixture to lighten it, then fold in the balance—lightly but thoroughly.

$\mathcal{S}$poon all into the prepared soufflé dish and bake, uncovered, in the preheated oven for 1 hour or until the pudding is set (it will be quite firm) and nicely browned. Remove the pudding from the oven and cool upright for 10 minutes. Very carefully loosen the pudding around the edge with a thin-bladed knife or small spatula, then invert on a large round plate. Place the confectioners' sugar in a small fine sieve and dust it over the top of the pudding. Cut into wedges at once and serve as is or topped with one of the sauces suggested in the recipe headnote.

$\mathcal{P}$LANTATION SWEET POTATO PUDDING

MAKES 8 SERVINGS

6 cups finely grated raw sweet potatoes
(about 1½ pounds)

¾ cup evaporated skim milk

¾ cup water

½ cup liquid egg substitute

¼ cup molasses

½ cup minced mixed candied fruits

⅓ cup minced crystallized ginger

2 tablespoons butter flavor granules

Finely grated zest of 1 orange

Finely grated zest of 1 lemon

1 teaspoon ground cinnamon

½ teaspoon freshly grated nutmeg

¼ teaspoon vanilla

TOPPING:

Mock Whipped Cream (page 174) or
Labna (page 176)

PER SERVING: 265 C   6 g P   0.4 g TF
(0.1 g SAT)   60 g CARB   264 mg S
2.2 mg CH

$\mathcal{I}$f this pudding is to have the proper texture, you must grate the sweet potatoes quite fine, bake the pudding long and slow, and stir it several times as it bakes.

$\mathcal{P}$reheat the oven to moderately slow (325° F.). Mix all ingredients together in a large bowl, then pour into a 6-cup flameproof casserole sprayed with nonstick vegetable cooking spray. Bake, uncovered, in the preheated oven for 2 hours, stirring well every ½ hour to redistribute the potatoes. Transfer to the broiler, about 4 inches from the heat, and broil 1 to 2 minutes or until tipped with brown. Serve topped with dollops of Mock Whipped Cream or Labna.

$\mathcal{T}$IPSY PARSON

MAKES 12 SERVINGS

CUSTARD:

⅓ cup superfine sugar

3 tablespoons cornstarch

1¾ cups whole milk

¼ cup evaporated skim milk

1½ teaspoons unsalted soft tub margarine (not extra-light)

¾ cup liquid egg substitute

¼ cup Malmsey (sweet Madeira wine)

APRICOT MIXTURE:

2 (1-pound) cans peeled apricot halves, drained well and puréed

2 tablespoons superfine sugar

¼ teaspoon almond extract

FOR PREPARING THE CAKE PANS:

Nonstick vegetable cooking spray

1 tablespoon unsalted soft tub margarine (not extra-light)

2 rounded tablespoons all-purpose flour

$\mathcal{T}$his English trifle will wow dinner guests, especially when they learn how low it is in cholesterol. Made the old-fashioned way, trifles are loaded with egg yolks and heavy cream, but this pared-down version is equally glamorous and delicious. It substitutes angel food cake for the traditional yellow sponge or pound cake, a virtually cholesterol-less custard for the usual egg-rich one, and a fluffy fake whipped cream for the real thing. It is long-winded but it can be made in stages, most of them well ahead of time. Note: You can make things even easier by using an angel food cake mix instead of the from-scratch recipe below, although its taste and texture won't be as good. Use 1 package (the 14.5-ounce size) of low-sodium angel food cake mix and prepare the batter according to the package label. Divide between the 2 prepared jelly-roll pans and bake for 20 minutes in a moderately slow oven (325° F.). Once the 2 cakes are done, proceed as the recipe directs.

$\mathcal{P}$repare the Custard First: Combine the sugar and cornstarch in a medium-size heavy saucepan, stir in the whole milk and evaporated skim milk, add the margarine, set over moderate heat, and cook, stirring constantly, about 3 minutes until thickened and smooth. Place the egg substitute in a medium-size heatproof bowl, quickly bring the cornstarch mixture to a boil, then very slowly pour it into the egg substitute, whisking hard all the while. Note: Take care that you don't add the cornstarch mixture too fast because the egg substitute may curdle. If it should, despite all precautions, simply put the finished custard through a fine sieve. Stir in the Malmsey and cool 30 minutes, whisking often to prevent a skin from forming on the surface of the custard. Cover and refrigerate until needed. Note: The custard can be made a day ahead of time.

$\mathcal{F}$or the Apricot Mixture: Combine all ingredients in a small nonmetallic bowl, cover, and chill until needed. Note: This mixture can also be made well ahead of time.

CAKE:

---

9 jumbo egg whites

¼ teaspoon cream of tartar

⅛ teaspoon salt

1 cup plus 2 tablespoons sifted
granulated sugar

1 cup plus 2 tablespoons sifted
cake flour

1 tablespoon freshly squeezed
lemon juice

1½ teaspoons vanilla

½ teaspoon almond extract

6 tablespoons confectioners' sugar

½ cup sieved red raspberry jam

⅓ cup Malmsey (sweet Madeira wine)

GARNISHES:

---

1 recipe Mock Whipped Cream
(page 174)

6 to 8 perfect whole raspberries or
2 large ripe apricots or 1 large ripe
nectarine or peach, peeled, pitted, and
sliced thin

3 sprigs mint, lemon verbena, or rose
geranium

PER SERVING: 348 C   9 g P   2.8 g TF (1 g
SAT)   70 g CARB   141 mg S   5.7 mg CH

To Prepare the Cake Pans: Spray the bottoms of 2 (15½ × 10½ × 1-inch) jelly-roll pans lightly with the nonstick spray, then smooth a cut-to-fit piece of baking parchment or wax paper over the bottom of each pan. Grease the parchment and pan sides evenly with the margarine, add the flour, and tilt the pans from side to side until the parchment and pan sides are evenly filmed with flour. Tap out the excess flour and set the pans aside.

For the Cake: Preheat the oven to slow (300° F.). Beat the egg whites at moderately slow electric mixer speed with the cream of tartar and salt until frothy. With the mixer still running, add the granulated sugar, 1 tablespoon at a time. When all of it has been incorporated, continue beating to *very soft* peaks. Now sift 2 tablespoons of the flour over the whites and fold in gently using a flat wire whisk or large rubber spatula. Continue folding in the balance of the flour the same way, 2 tablespoons at a time. Fold in the lemon juice, vanilla, and almond extract. *Note: Use the lightest touch possible at all times lest you knock the air out of the beaten whites.*

Divide the batter between the 2 prepared pans, smoothing it evenly into the corners. Bake about 25 minutes in the preheated oven, reversing the position of the pans at halftime, until the cakes are springy to the touch. They will be pale, but don't bake any longer or they will toughen. Meanwhile, spread 2 kitchen towels on the counter and sift the confectioners' sugar over each to cover an area a little larger than that of 1 cake.

The instant you take the cakes from the oven, invert on the sugared towels and peel off the parchment. Using a sharp serrated knife, trim from one of the cakes any crisp edges that might crack when the cake is rolled. With one of the short ends toward you, roll this cake up in the towel and let it cool 30 minutes. Cover the remaining cake loosely with a kitchen towel and cool 30 minutes.

*U*nroll the rolled-up cake, spread it evenly with the raspberry jam, leaving ½ inch margins all around, then reroll, jelly-roll style, and let stand, covered by the towel, 20 minutes. Meanwhile, prick the second cake evenly all over with a table fork and sprinkle evenly with the Malmsey. Let stand, uncovered, for 20 minutes. Remove the towel from the jelly-roll cake and sift any loose confectioners' sugar over it. Cut the wine-soaked cake into 1-inch cubes.

To Assemble the Tipsy Parson: Pour about 1 cup of the apricot mixture into the bottom of a 2½- to 3-quart crystal bowl (I like to use an outsize brandy snifter because it shows the dessert off so dramatically), then add about 2 cups of the cake cubes. Now very carefully cut enough of the jelly roll into ⅜-inch slices to stand on end in a single row around the sides of the bowl (wipe your knife between each cut so you don't smear jam all over the slices). Press the slices lightly against the sides of the bowl and support them as needed with additional cake cubes. Pour about ¾ cup of the custard over the cake cubes in the center of the bowl, then ½ cup of the apricot mixture. Stand a second row of jelly-roll slices inside and about halfway above the first row, again pressing lightly against the sides of the bowl and propping them by piling more of the cake cubes in the middle of the bowl. Add another ¾ cup of custard and ½ cup of the apricot mixture, then the remaining cake cubes, mounding them up in the middle of the bowl. Top with the remaining apricot mixture, then the remaining custard, spooning it in carefully so that it doesn't run down the sides of the bowl and obscure the jelly-roll slices. Cover the Tipsy Parson and let it stand in the refrigerator at least 2 hours.

Just before serving, drift the Mock Whipped Cream on top of the Tipsy Parson, swirling it into peaks and valleys, then add a cluster of raspberries or wreathe with apricot slices and sprig with mint.

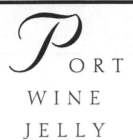

$\mathcal{P}$ORT
WINE
JELLY

MAKES 6 SERVINGS

2 envelopes unflavored gelatin

¾ cup superfine sugar

2 cups water

1 (2 × ½-inch) strip lemon zest

1 small cinnamon stick, broken in half

2½ cups vintage port or Malmsey or
Bual (sweet Madeira wines)

1 recipe Mock Whipped Cream (page
174)

PER SERVING: 291 C   4 g P   0 g TF (0 g
SAT)   42 g CARB   43 mg S   0.9 mg CH

This jelly must chill for 24 hours, so plan accordingly.

Combine the gelatin and sugar in a small heavy saucepan, mix in the water, then drop in the lemon zest and cinnamon stick. Set over moderate heat and cook and stir about 5 minutes until the gelatin dissolves completely. Cool to room temperature, then remove and discard the lemon zest and cinnamon stick. Carefully mix in the port, pour into a large nonmetallic bowl, cover, and chill 24 hours or until set. To serve, layer in crystal goblets or parfait glasses, alternating with spoonfuls of Mock Whipped Cream.

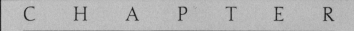

CHAPTER

3

TARTS,
PIES,
AND
PASTRIES

$\mathcal{L}$OW-
CHOLESTEROL
PIECRUST

MAKES ENOUGH FOR A 9- OR 10-
INCH PIE OR TART SHELL PLUS
ENOUGH EXTRA FOR SMALL DECO-
RATIVE "TOP CRUST" CUTOUTS
(8 SERVINGS)

1 cup sifted cornstarch
⅔ cup sifted all-purpose flour
1 tablespoon sugar
1 teaspoon butter flavor granules
½ teaspoon finely grated lemon zest
5 tablespoons extra-light olive oil or
vegetable oil (canola, safflower,
sunflower, corn oil, etc.)
¼ cup cold water
1 tablespoon liquid egg substitute

PER SERVING: (WITHOUT "TOP CRUST"
CUTOUTS): 115 C 1 g P 5.6 g TF (0.6 g
AT) 15 g CARB 10 mg S 0 mg CH

PER SERVING (WITH "TOP CRUST"
CUTOUTS): 174 C 1 g P 8.5 g TF (0.9
g SAT) 23 g CARB 15 mg S 0 mg CH

$\mathcal{T}$he texture of this pastry is more like that of a cookie or cracker than that of a conventional piecrust—firm-crisp rather than flaky. To keep it crisp, partially bake the crust and cool to room temperature before you fill it. And if the filling is extra moist, bake the crust fully and let it air-dry before adding the filling. The trimmings can be rerolled, cut into fancy shapes, then baked and laid on the finished pie to add a festive touch.

$\mathcal{P}$reheat the oven to moderately hot (375° F.). Mix the cornstarch, flour, sugar, butter granules, and lemon zest thoroughly in a large shallow bowl. Whisk the oil with the water and egg substitute in a 2-cup measure until creamy. Drizzle over the cornstarch mixture, then fork briskly until crumbly. If not all the dry ingredients are moistened, work the mixture *lightly* with your hands until uniformly crumbly. Gather the pastry into a ball, place on a 12-inch square of wax paper, then flatten with your hands into a thick round about 6 inches in diameter. Top with a second square of wax paper, set on a slightly dampened counter, then, with short, quick strokes, roll the pastry from the center outward into a circle about 3 inches larger in diameter than the pie pan you are using.

$\mathcal{C}$arefully peel off the top piece of paper, center the pie pan upside-down on the pastry, then, using the bottom sheet of wax paper for support, quickly but gently invert the pan and the pastry together—the pastry will ease into the pan. Now, gently peel off the remaining sheet of wax paper and pat the pastry against the bottom and sides of the pan, making sure there are no cracks or holes (if there are, simply pinch together firmly to seal or patch with some of the pastry trimmings, patting these securely into place). Trim the pastry overhang so that it is about ½ inch larger all around than the pie pan, then roll the edges under until they rest on the rim of the pan and crimp, making a fluted edge. Prick the bottom and sides of the crust well with the tines of a fork. *Note: It's not necessary to weight this pie shell before you bake it. It will not shrink the way a conventional crust does.*

To Partially Bake the Pie Shell: Bake for 15 minutes in the lower two thirds of the preheated oven until pale tan and crisp, then cool on a wire rack for at least 30 minutes before filling.

To Fully Bake the Pie Shell: Bake for 20 to 25 minutes in the lower two thirds of the preheated oven until lightly browned and crisp, then cool on a wire rack for at least 30 minutes before filling.

For Decorative "Top-Crust" Cutouts: Gather the trimmings into a ball and roll about ⅛ inch thick between 2 pieces of wax paper. Very carefully peel off the top piece of wax paper, place a baking sheet on top of the pastry, then, using the bottom sheet of wax paper for support, invert. Carefully peel off the top piece of wax paper and, using small star, heart, crescent, or other fancy cutters measuring ½ to 1½ inches across, make the cutouts right on the baking sheet and peel away the trimmings. Bake for 12 to 15 minutes in the middle of the preheated oven, then cool, and arrange decoratively on the pie filling. If you prefer a more "baked-on" look, arrange the baked cutouts on the fillings about 5 minutes before the pie comes from the oven.

VEGETABLE OIL PASTRY

MAKES ENOUGH FOR AN 8- OR 9-INCH PIE OR TART SHELL (6 TO 8 SERVINGS)

1¼ cups unsifted all-purpose flour
Pinch of salt
⅓ cup extra-light olive oil or vegetable oil (canola, safflower, sunflower, corn oil, etc.)
2 to 3 tablespoons ice water

PER SERVING: 200–150 C   3–2 g P   12.6–9.4 g TF   (1.8–1.4 g SAT)   20–15 g CARB   22–17 mg S   0–0 mg CH

Sift the flour and salt into a medium-size bowl. Whisk the oil and 2 tablespoons of the ice water until creamy and slightly thickened. Dump into the flour mixture, and fork briskly to blend. If the pastry seems dry, fork in the remaining tablespoon of ice water. Pat the pastry into a ball, place on a 12-inch square of wax paper, then flatten with your hands into a thick round about 6 inches in diameter. Top with a second square of wax paper, set on a slightly dampened counter, and roll the pastry into a circle 3 inches larger than the pie pan you're using—an 11-inch circle for an 8-inch pan, a 12-inch circle for a 9-inch pan. Peel off the top sheet of wax paper, carefully invert the pastry on the pie pan, and peel off the second sheet of wax paper. Trim the overhang so that it is 1 inch larger than the pan, then roll the edge under even with the pan rim and crimp, making a high fluted edge. The pastry is now ready to fill and bake as individual recipes direct.

For a Baked Pie Shell: Preheat the oven to moderate (350° F.). Prick the bottom and sides of the pie shell with a fork, line the shell with aluminum foil, and fill with pie weights or dried beans. Bake 15 minutes in the preheated oven, remove the foil and weights, and bake 15 to 20 minutes longer, until pale tan and crisp.

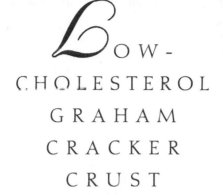

Low-Cholesterol Graham Cracker Crust

MAKES ENOUGH FOR A 9- OR 10-INCH SPRINGFORM PAN (UP TO 24 SERVINGS)

⚖

2½ cups graham cracker crumbs (you'll need about 20 double crackers, each 4½ × 2¼ inches)

3 tablespoons sugar

1 tablespoon butter flavor granules

4 tablespoons extra-light olive oil or vegetable oil (canola, safflower, sunflower, corn oil, etc.) blended with 3 tablespoons evaporated skim milk

PER SERVING: 79 C 1 g P 3.2 g TF (0.3 g SAT) 11 g CARB 99 mg S 0.2 mg CH

Preheat the oven to moderate (350° F.). Combine the crumbs, sugar, and butter granules, sprinkle the oil mixture evenly over all, and toss thoroughly to mix, or buzz about 10 seconds in a food processor. Pat the mixture over the bottom and up the sides of a 9-inch springform pan or over the bottom and halfway up the sides of a 10-inch springform pan. Using the back of a spoon, pat the mixture firmly into place. Bake, uncovered, 8 to 10 minutes in the preheated oven, then cool to room temperature before filling.

VARIATIONS:

♣ *Spicy Low-Cholesterol Graham Cracker Crust for a 9- or 10-Inch Springform Pan (up to 24 servings):* Add ½ teaspoon each ground cinnamon and ginger and ¼ teaspoon each ground cloves and freshly grated nutmeg or ground mace to the crumb mixture and proceed as directed.

PER SERVING: 79 C 1 g P 3.2 g TF (0.3 g SAT) 11 g CARB 99 mg S 0.2 mg CH

♣ *Low-Cholesterol Graham Cracker Crust for a 9-Inch Pie Pan (up to 12 servings):* Prepare as directed using 2 cups graham cracker crumbs, 2 tablespoons sugar, 2 teaspoons butter flavor granules, and 4 tablespoons oil blended with 1½ tablespoons liquid egg substitute.

PER SERVING: 131 C 2 g P 6 g TF (0.7 g SAT) 17 g CARB 151 mg S 0.1 mg CH

♣ *Spicy Low-Cholesterol Graham Cracker Crust for a 9-Inch Pie Pan (up to 12 servings):* Prepare the crumb crust for the 9-inch pie pan as directed but add ¼ teaspoon each ground cinnamon and ginger, and ⅛ teaspoon each ground cloves and freshly grated nutmeg or ground mace.

PER SERVING: 131 C 2 g P 6 g TF (0.7 g SAT) 17 g CARB 151 mg S 0.1 mg CH

Low-
CHOLESTEROL
CHEESE
PIE

MAKES 24 SERVINGS

CRUST:

1 recipe Low-Cholesterol Graham
Cracker Crust (see page 67)

FILLING:

2 (8-ounce) cartons no-cholesterol
vegetable-based cream cheese substitute
(see page xvii)

2 cups lowfat (1 percent) cottage cheese

1 cup no-cholesterol vegetable-based sour
cream substitute (see page xix)

¾ cup sugar

⅔ cup liquid egg substitute

1½ teaspoons vanilla

TOPPING:

1 cup no-cholesterol vegetable-based sour
cream substitute

⅓ cup sugar

1 teaspoon vanilla

*F*ood science has made it easy for cholesterol-counters to enjoy rich, creamy desserts. For example, this devastating cheese pie is no longer off-limits thanks to vegetable-based sour cream and cream cheese substitutes. Most supermarkets stock both in their dairy counters. Read the labels carefully, however, to make sure that the mock sour cream or mock cream cheese you buy is truly cholesterol-free and low in saturated fats.

For the Crust: Prepare the graham cracker crust as directed, reserving 1 tablespoon of the crumb mixture, if you like, to use in garnishing the cheese pie. Pat the remaining crumb mixture over the bottom and halfway up the sides of a 10-inch springform pan, but do not bake. Preheat the oven to moderately slow (325° F.).

For the Filling: Churn all ingredients in a food processor 1 to 1½ minutes until absolutely smooth. Or beat at highest electric mixer speed until smooth. Pour into the prepared piecrust, set on a baking sheet, and bake 35 minutes in the preheated oven. Remove from the oven and let stand at room temperature 10 minutes. Also raise the oven temperature to hot (400° F.).

Meanwhile, Prepare the Topping: Quickly whisk all topping ingredients together and, when the pie has cooled 10 minutes, pour over the filling. Using a rubber spatula, spread the topping carefully and smoothly so that it covers the filling completely and touches the crust all around. Return the pie to the oven and bake 10 minutes. Remove from the oven and cool the pie in its pan on a wire rack for 1 hour. Set, uncovered, in the refrigerator and chill at least 8 hours or overnight. Carefully release the springform pan sides and remove. If you have opted for the Garnish, sprinkle the reserved crumb mixture over the top of the cheese pie, then cut the pie into slim wedges.

OPTIONAL GARNISH:

1 tablespoon Low-Cholesterol Graham Cracker Crust crumb mixture (see Crust, above)

PER SERVING: 202 C   6 g P   10 g TF
(2.1 g SAT)   23 g CARB   254 mg S
0.9 mg CH

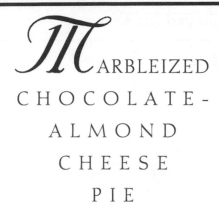

MARBLEIZED CHOCOLATE-ALMOND CHEESE PIE

MAKES 24 SERVINGS

CRUST:

2½ cups graham cracker crumbs (you'll need about 20 double crackers, each 4½ × 2¼ inches)

¼ cup sugar

3 tablespoons unsweetened Dutch process cocoa powder

1 tablespoon butter flavor granules

5 tablespoons extra-light olive oil or vegetable oil (canola, safflower, sunflower, corn oil, etc.) blended with 2 tablespoons liquid egg substitute

FILLING:

3½ ounces marzipan, cut into small dice

1 (8-ounce) carton no-cholesterol vegetable-based cream cheese substitute (see page xvii)

2 cups lowfat (1 percent) cottage cheese

1 cup no-cholesterol vegetable-based sour cream substitute (see page xix)

¾ cup sugar

1 tablespoon melted unsalted soft tub margarine (not extra-light)

Note: Toward the end of baking, the filling may puff above the level of the crust, even crack a bit around the edges. No matter. On cooling, it will fall back into place and the cracks will vanish.

For the Crust: Combine all ingredients well and pat over the bottom and halfway up the sides of a 10-inch springform pan; set aside. Preheat the oven to moderately slow (325° F.).

For the Filling: Churn all ingredients except the egg substitute and cocoa in a food processor about 2 minutes until absolutely smooth. Add the egg substitute and pulse 3 to 4 times to incorporate. Transfer ½ the filling to a medium-size bowl, then spoon about 1 cup of this into a smaller bowl and blend in the cocoa. Stir back into the medium-size bowl and whisk well to mix. Set the springform pan on a baking sheet, ladle ½ cup of the white filling into the crust (it is quite thick and will not flatten out), then, beside it, ladle ½ cup of the chocolate filling. Repeat, moving in a circular direction around the crust without stirring, until you have used up all the filling. Using a thin-bladed spatula and starting about 1 inch in from the edge of the pan, draw 3 concentric circles—clockwise, counterclockwise, clockwise—in the filling, about 1 inch apart, to marbleize. Do not stir or you'll have chocolate pie.

Bake 1¼ hours in the preheated oven or until a toothpick inserted midway between the crust and the center comes out clean. Remove from the oven and let stand at room temperature 1 hour. Set, uncovered, in the refrigerator and chill at least 4 hours. Carefully release the springform pan sides and remove, then cut the pie into slim wedges.

1½ teaspoons vanilla
¼ teaspoon almond extract
¾ cup liquid egg substitute
3 tablespoons unsweetened Dutch
process cocoa powder

PER SERVING: 186 C 5 g P 8 g TF (1.6 g
SAT) 24 g CARB 228 mg S 0.8 mg CH

V A R I A T I O N :

 Chocolate Velvet Cheese Pie (24 servings): Prepare the filling as directed but increase the vanilla to 2 teaspoons, omit the almond extract, and churn the cocoa with all the other filling ingredients except the egg substitute. Pulse in the egg substitute as above, pour the filling into the prepared crust, bake and chill as directed.

PER SERVING: 186 C 5 g P 8 g TF (1.6 g SAT) 24 g CARB 228 mg S 0.8 mg CH

GLAZED ORANGE TOFU CHEESECAKE

MAKES 24 SERVINGS

CRUST:

1 recipe Spicy Low-Cholesterol Graham Cracker Crust for a 9- or 10-Inch Springform Pan (page 67)

FILLING:

2 (1-pound) packages soft tofu, drained as dry as possible and cubed

½ cup firmly packed dark brown sugar

1¼ cups orange marmalade

¾ cup no-cholesterol vegetable-based sour cream substitute (see page xix)

¼ cup no-cholesterol vegetable-based cream cheese substitute (see page xvii)

2 tablespoons melted unsalted soft tub margarine (not extra-light)

¼ cup Grand Marnier

1 tablespoon finely grated orange zest

1 cup liquid egg substitute

GLAZE:

1 tablespoon cornstarch

1 tablespoon freshly squeezed lemon juice

¾ cup orange marmalade

PER SERVING: 222 C   4 g P   6.4 g TF   (0.8 g SAT)   37 g CARB   130 mg S   0.2 mg CH

Let me be up-front about this cheesecake. My tofu-loving friends adore it, but others less fond of the taste and texture of soy bean curd aren't so sure until the third or fourth bite. By then, most of them have come round and pronounce it delicious. But I have to say that there have been a couple of hold-outs who prefer the richness and smoothness of my *Low-Cholesterol Cheese Pie* (page 68) and *Marbleized Chocolate-Almond Cheese Pie* (page 70).

For the Crust: Prepare the graham cracker crust as directed, pat over the bottom and halfway up the sides of a 10-inch springform pan, but do not bake. Preheat the oven to moderately slow (325° F.).

For the Filling: Churn all ingredients except the egg substitute in a food processor about 2 minutes until absolutely smooth. Add the egg substitute and pulse 3 to 4 times to incorporate. Pour into the prepared piecrust, set on a baking sheet, and bake 1¼ hours in the preheated oven until a tooth-pick inserted midway between the crust and the center comes out clean. Remove from the oven and cool 1 hour on a wire rack.

Meanwhile, Prepare the Glaze: In a small heavy saucepan, combine the cornstarch and lemon juice, then blend in the marmalade. Set over moderate heat and cook, whisking constantly, 3 to 4 minutes until the mixture bubbles up, thickens, and clears. Cool to room temperature.

When the cheesecake is cool, carefully release and remove the springform pan sides and remove any loose crumbs that may have fallen onto the filling. Spoon the glaze onto the cheesecake, then, using the back of the spoon, gently smooth it evenly over the filling.

Set the cheesecake, uncovered, in the refrigerator and chill at least 24 hours. Cut into slim wedges and serve.

The Soufflé for
Chocoholics *(page 52)*

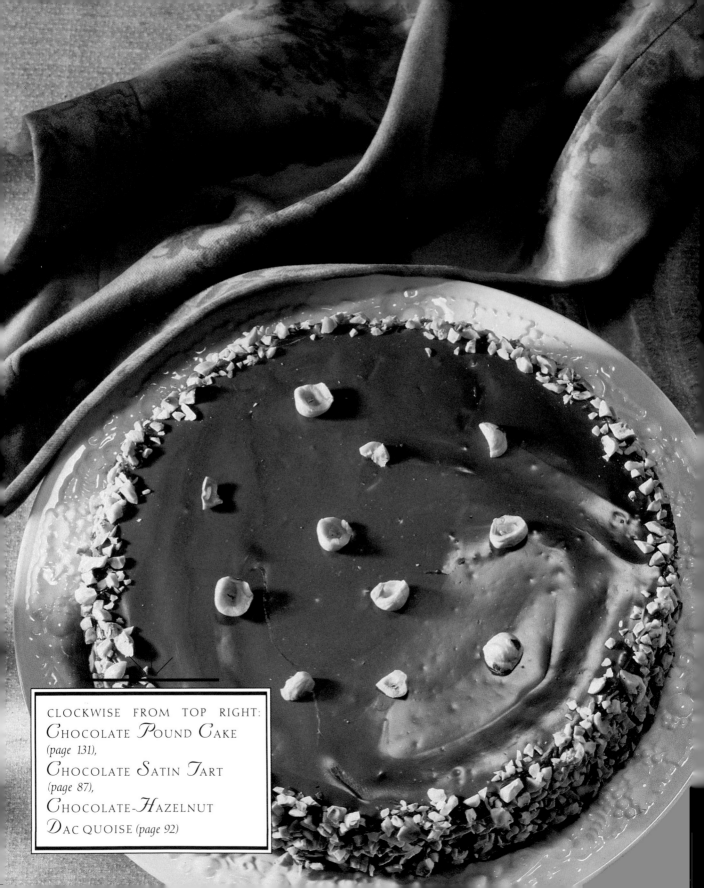

CLOCKWISE FROM TOP RIGHT:
Chocolate Pound Cake
(page 131),
Chocolate Satin Tart
(page 87),
Chocolate-Hazelnut
Dacquoise (page 92)

RASPBERRY-STRAWBERRY
VACHERIN (page 20)

S PICY PUMPKIN PIE WITH GRAND MARNIER

MAKES 8 SERVINGS

PASTRY:

1 recipe Low-Cholesterol Piecrust (page 64)

FILLING:

½ cup firmly packed light brown sugar

¼ cup granulated sugar

1 tablespoon finely grated orange zest

¾ teaspoon ground cinnamon

½ teaspoon ground ginger

½ teaspoon freshly grated nutmeg

⅛ teaspoon ground cloves

1 tablespoon Grand Marnier

½ cup liquid egg substitute

1¼ cups evaporated skim milk

1 (1-pound) can solid-pack pumpkin (not pumpkin pie mix)

PER SERVING: 252 C   6 g P   5.8 g TF (0.7 g SAT)   45 g CARB   83 mg S   1.7 mg CH

*F*reshly grated nutmeg has a delicate fruity flavor that the commercially ground spice cannot match.

For the Pastry: Preheat the oven to moderately hot (375° F.). Prepare and roll the pastry as directed, fit it into a 9-inch pie pan, making a high fluted edge, then partially bake and cool 30 minutes. Reduce the oven temperature to moderately slow (325° F.)

For the Filling: Combine all ingredients, beating until smooth. Set the piecrust on a baking sheet, pour in the filling, and bake about 1 hour or until set. Cool the pie to room temperature before cutting.

OLD-FASHIONED LEMON CHESS PIE

MAKES 8 SERVINGS

PASTRY:

1 recipe Low-Cholesterol Piecrust (page 64) or Vegetable Oil Pastry (page 66)

FILLING:

1 cup sugar

2 tablespoons cornstarch

1 tablespoon finely grated lemon zest

1 cup liquid egg substitute

⅓ cup freshly squeezed lemon juice

2 tablespoons extra-light olive oil or vegetable oil (canola, safflower, sunflower, corn oil, etc.)

PER SERVING: 264 C   4 g P   9 g TF (1.1 g SAT)   44 g CARB   50 mg S   0 mg CH

When making Lemon Chess Pie, traditionalists don't stint on butter or eggs. I've eliminated both in this low-cholesterol version and come up with a recipe that's both rich and delicious.

For the Pastry: Prepare and roll the pastry as directed, fit it into a 9-inch pie pan, making a high fluted edge, but do not bake. Preheat the oven to moderately slow (325° F.).

For the Filling: Blend the sugar with the cornstarch and lemon zest, then stir in the egg substitute and lemon juice. Add the oil in a fine stream, stirring all the while, and do not stop stirring until it is completely incorporated. This is important. If you don't mix the oil in thoroughly, the filling is apt to separate during baking.

Set the piecrust on a baking sheet, pour in the filling, and bake 40 to 45 minutes in the preheated oven, just until the filling is lightly puffed and quivers only slightly when you nudge the pie pan. Cool to room temperature before cutting. *Note: The filling will fall as it cools, but this is the nature of all chess pies.*

PLANTATION PECAN PIE

MAKES 8 SERVINGS

PASTRY:

1 recipe Low-Cholesterol Piecrust (page 64) or Vegetable Oil Pastry (page 66)

FILLING:

¾ cup firmly packed light or dark brown sugar

2 tablespoons cornstarch

⅛ teaspoon salt

3 egg whites

½ cup evaporated skim milk

2 teaspoons freshly squeezed lemon juice

1½ teaspoons vanilla

2 tablespoons extra-light olive oil or vegetable oil (canola, safflower, sunflower, corn oil, etc.)

¾ cup coarsely chopped pecans

PER SERVING: 350 C   5 g P   16.6 g TF (1.9 g SAT)   41 g CARB   90 mg S   0.7 mg CH

*W*ho would have thought that most of the cholesterol and saturated fat could be subtracted from this killer pie? The old Southern way to make it is with plenty of butter and egg yolks.

For the Pastry: Prepare and roll the pastry as directed, fit it into a 9-inch pie pan, making a high fluted edge, but do not bake. Preheat the oven to moderately slow (325° F.).

For the Filling: Blend the sugar with the cornstarch and salt, then beat in the egg whites, one by one. Stir in the milk, lemon juice, and vanilla. Add the oil in a fine stream, stirring all the while, and do not stop stirring until it is completely incorporated. This is important. If you don't mix the oil in thoroughly, the filling is apt to separate during baking. Finally, stir in the pecans.

*S*et the piecrust on a baking sheet, pour in the filling, and bake 40 to 45 minutes in the preheated oven, just until the filling is lightly set and puffed (it may have cracked a bit, too, but this is par for pecan pies). Cool at least 1 hour before cutting. *Note: The filling will fall as it cools but this is as it should be.*

FRESH GINGER AND WALNUT PIE

MAKES 8 SERVINGS

PASTRY:

1 recipe Low-Cholesterol Piecrust (page 64) or Vegetable Oil Pastry (page 66)

FILLING:

¾ cup firmly packed light brown sugar

⅓ cup finely chopped fresh ginger

2 tablespoons cornstarch

1 tablespoon finely grated orange zest

2 tablespoons extra-light olive oil or vegetable oil (canola, safflower, sunflower, corn oil, etc.)

3 egg whites

1 tablespoon freshly squeezed lemon juice

½ cup evaporated skim milk

⅔ cup coarsely chopped walnuts

PER SERVING: 316 C   5 g P   15.2 g TF (1.6 g SAT)   42 g CARB   57 mg S   0.7 mg CH

When you make this pie, be sure that the walnuts are good and fresh, otherwise the pie will take on a rancid flavor. If you have a food processor, you can buzz up the filling in less than 5 minutes.

For the Pastry: Prepare and roll the pastry as directed, fit it into a 9-inch pie pan, making a high fluted edge, but do not bake. Preheat the oven to moderately slow (325° F.).

For the Filling: Combine the brown sugar, ginger, cornstarch, orange zest, and oil, creaming until smooth (or churn in a food processor about 60 seconds). Beat (or pulse) in the egg whites, one by one, then mix (or pulse) in the lemon juice, milk, and walnuts.

Set the piecrust on a baking sheet, pour in the filling, and bake 40 to 45 minutes in the preheated oven, just until the filling is lightly set and puffed. Cool at least 1 hour before cutting. *Note: The filling will fall as it cools but this is as it should be.*

O S L O
A P P L E
P I E

MAKES 8 SERVINGS

½ cup unsifted all-purpose flour

½ cup firmly packed dark brown sugar

¼ cup granulated sugar

1 teaspoon baking powder

¼ teaspoon freshly grated nutmeg

¼ teaspoon ground cardamom

2 teaspoons butter flavor granules

½ cup liquid egg substitute

1 cup moderately coarsely chopped, peeled and cored apple (about 1 large Rome Beauty)

½ cup moderately coarsely chopped pecans or walnuts

1 teaspoon vanilla

TOPPING:

1 recipe Mock Whipped Cream (page 174)

PER SERVING: 181 C   3 g P   4.7 g TF (0.4 g SAT)   32 g CARB   132 mg S   0.5 mg CH

A moist crustless pie that contains no fat other than that in the nuts.

Preheat the oven to moderate (350° F.). Spray the bottom and sides of a 9-inch pie pan with nonstick vegetable cooking spray and set aside. Place the flour, brown and granulated sugars, baking powder, nutmeg, cardamom, and butter granules in a food processor (or in an electric blender) and pulse 8 to 10 times to mix. Add all remaining ingredients except the topping and pulse 8 to 10 times more to combine—the mixture should be lumpy. Pour into the prepared pie pan and bake, uncovered, in the preheated oven for 30 minutes. Remove the pie from the oven and cool in the upright pan on a wire rack for 30 minutes. Cut into wedges, top each portion with a generous dollop of Mock Whipped Cream, and serve.

DATE-OATMEAL MACAROON PIE

MAKES 8 SERVINGS

¾ cup sugar

1 tablespoon cornstarch

1 teaspoon baking powder

½ cup coarsely chopped pecans or walnuts

½ cup quick-cooking rolled oats

3 extra-large egg whites

1 teaspoon freshly squeezed lemon juice

1 teaspoon vanilla

½ teaspoon almond extract

½ cup finely diced pitted dates

OPTIONAL TOPPING:

Mock Whipped Cream (page 174)

PER SERVING: 186 C   3 g P   5.4 g TF (0.5 g SAT)   33 g CARB   78 mg S   0 mg CH

Here's another no-crust pie. This one is crackly on top, creamy inside.

Preheat the oven to moderately slow (325° F.). Spray a 9-inch pie pan with nonstick vegetable cooking spray, dust lightly with flour, then set aside. Mix the sugar, cornstarch, baking powder, pecans, and rolled oats in a small bowl and set aside also. Beat the egg whites with the lemon juice to stiff, glossy peaks, fold in the vanilla and almond extract, then the sugar mixture. Finally, fold in the dates and spoon into the prepared pan.

Bake, uncovered in the preheated oven for 30 minutes, until puffed and lightly browned, then cool on a wire rack for 45 minutes (the pie will fall slightly but this is as it should be). Cut into wedges and top, if you like, with Mock Whipped Cream.

STAR-SPANGLED CRANBERRY-APPLE TART

MAKES 8 SERVINGS

PASTRY:

1 recipe Low-Cholesterol Piecrust (page 64)

2 teaspoons sugar (glaze)

FILLING:

1 (12-ounce) package cranberries, stemmed and sorted

2 medium-size sweet apples such as Rome Beauties, peeled, cored, and coarsely chopped

1⅓ cups sugar

¼ cup apple cider

1 teaspoon vanilla

PER SERVING: 350 C 2 g P 8.6 g TF (0.9 g SAT) 70 g CARB 16 mg S 0.1 mg CH

Perfect for Thanksgiving.

For the Pastry: Preheat the oven to moderately hot (375° F.). Prepare the piecrust as the recipe directs, roll and fit it into a 9-inch tart tin that has a removable bottom; trim off and reserve the pastry overhang. Bake the tart shell fully as directed, then cool for 30 minutes. Meanwhile, roll the pastry trimmings, cut into ½-, 1- and/or 2-inch stars, sprinkle with the 2 teaspoons sugar, and bake as directed but for 5 minutes only. Cool and reserve. Reduce the oven temperature to 350° F.

For the Filling: Mix the cranberries, apples, sugar, and cider in a heavy medium-size saucepan and bring to a boil over moderate heat. Adjust the heat so the mixture bubbles gently and simmer, uncovered, for 10 minutes or until the cranberries have popped and the mixture is the consistency of applesauce. Cool to room temperature and stir in the vanilla.

Spoon the cranberry mixture into the tart shell and set on a 15½ × 10½ × 1-inch jelly-roll pan. Bake 15 minutes, arrange the pastry stars decoratively on top of the tart filling, then continue baking for 5 to 8 minutes more, or until the pastry stars are golden brown and the filling is bubbly. Cool the tart to room temperature on a wire rack, then carefully release the tart tin sides and remove. Slide the tart onto a decorative round platter and serve.

LITTLE LINZERS

MAKES 1½ DOZEN

1½ cups sifted cornstarch

¾ cup sifted all-purpose flour

1 cup sifted confectioners' sugar

1 cup very finely ground unblanched almonds

2 teaspoons finely grated lemon zest

1½ teaspoons ground cinnamon

½ teaspoon freshly grated nutmeg

½ teaspoon ground cloves

6 tablespoons extra-light olive oil or vegetable oil (canola, safflower, sunflower, corn oil, etc.)

6 tablespoons cold water

1 tablespoon liquid egg substitute

TOPPINGS:

½ cup sieved or seedless red raspberry jam

2 tablespoons sifted confectioners' sugar

PER LINZER: 176 C   2 g P   7.5 g TF (0.9 g SAT)   26 g CARB   4 mg S   0 mg CH

These are nothing more than crunchy cookies sandwiched together with raspberry jam, but the cutouts on top give them the look of little Linzertortes. Cut the rolled-out dough carefullly so you have a minimum of scraps to reroll. These rerolled Linzers will be tougher than the "first-rolls." Let the assembled Linzers stand several hours—or better yet, overnight—before serving so that the jam has a chance to seep in a bit and "glue" the tops and bottoms together.

Combine the cornstarch, flour, sugar, almonds, lemon zest, cinnamon, nutmeg, and cloves in a large shallow bowl. Next, place the oil, water, and egg substitute in a 2-cup measure and whisk until creamy. Drizzle the oil mixture over the dry ingredients, forking briskly all the while, and continue forking just until the mixture is uniformly moist and crumbly (it should hold together when you pinch a bit of it together). Shape the dough into a ball, flatten, wrap in wax paper, and chill for 1 hour. This makes the dough easier to roll.

When ready to proceed, preheat the oven to moderately hot (375° F.). With a lightly floured stockinette-covered rolling pin, roll the dough, ½ the total amount at a time, on a lightly floured pastry cloth until it is slightly thicker than a pie-crust—a little less than ¼ inch. Using a floured, fluted, 3-inch round cutter, cut into circles. Then, using smaller, fancily shaped cutters—hearts, stars, or little fluted rounds measuring about 1 inch across—cut the centers out of ½ the circles of dough. Space the cookies 1 inch apart on baking sheets lightly sprayed with nonstick vegetable cooking spray. Gather the cut-out centers and scraps of dough, reroll, cut, and place on the baking sheets.

Bake the cookies in the preheated oven for 12 to 15 minutes, or until soft-firm and very lightly ringed with tan. Transfer at once to wire racks and cool to room temperature.

To Assemble the Little Linzers: Turn each solid cookie upside-down and spread with the raspberry jam. Arrange the cookies with the cut-out centers on a wire rack, set on a counter covered with wax paper, then dust with the confectioners' sugar. Holding these cookies by the edges so as not to smudge the sugar, set on top of the jam-spread cookies to form little sandwiches. Allow the Linzers to stand for several hours before serving.

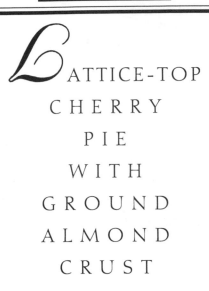

LATTICE-TOP CHERRY PIE WITH GROUND ALMOND CRUST

MAKES 8 SERVINGS

PASTRY:

1½ cups sifted cornstarch
¾ cup sifted all-purpose flour
¼ cup unsifted confectioners' sugar
¼ teaspoon baking powder
6 tablespoons finely ground unblanched almonds
1 teaspoon finely grated lemon zest
¼ cup extra-light olive oil or vegetable oil (canola, safflower, sunflower, corn oil, etc.)
2 tablespoons squeeze (liquid) margarine
6 tablespoons cold water
1 tablespoon liquid egg substitute
1 teaspoon vanilla

For the Pastry: Sift the cornstarch, flour, confectioners' sugar, and baking powder into a large bowl. Add the almonds and lemon zest and toss well to mix. Whisk the olive oil with the squeeze margarine, water, egg substitute, and vanilla in a 2-cup measure until creamy. Drizzle over the cornstarch mixture, then toss lightly with a fork until the pastry holds together. Don't overwork the pastry at this point or it will be tough. Shape gently into a ball, incorporating all crumbs in the bottom of the bowl, then flatten into a round about 2 inches thick. Wrap the pastry in plastic food wrap and let stand at room temperature for 30 minutes; this makes it easier to roll.

Roll ⅔ of the pastry between 2 sheets of floured wax paper into a 12-inch circle. Carefully peel off the top sheet of wax paper (if the pastry looks as if it will tear, refrigerate briefly to firm it up). Invert the pastry on a 9-inch pie pan, gently peel off the second sheet of wax paper, fit the pastry into the pan, trim the overhang so that it is 1 inch larger all around than the pie pan, then roll it over until even with the rim and crimp, leaving a high fluted edge. Set the pie shell in the refrigerator while you make the filling. Also chill the remaining pastry.

For the Filling: Mix the tapioca, sugar, cinnamon, allspice, and pepper in a large bowl. Add the cherries and Grand Marnier, toss to mix, and let stand 30 minutes at room temperature.

Place an oven rack in the lower third of the oven, slide a heavy baking sheet onto the rack, and preheat the oven to hot (425° F.). Spoon the cherry filling into the prepared pie shell and dot evenly with the margarine.

For the Lattice Top: Roll the remaining pastry between 2 sheets of floured wax paper into a 10-inch circle, then, using a very sharp knife dipped into cornstarch, cut into strips ½ inch wide. *Note: It will*

FILLING:

2 tablespoons quick-cooking tapioca
⅔ cup granulated sugar
¼ teaspoon ground cinnamon
⅛ teaspoon ground allspice
Pinch of freshly ground black pepper
4 cups drained, canned, pitted sour cherries
2 tablespoons Grand Marnier, Curaçao, or other orange liqueur
1½ tablespoons unsalted soft tub margarine (not extra-light)

PER SERVING: 439 C   3 g P   13.3 g TF (2 g SAT)   77 g CARB   48 mg S   0 mg CH

be easier to transfer the lattice top if you "weave" it on the bottom disc of a 10- or 12-inch springform pan that has been covered with wax paper. It will also be easier to transfer each strip to the springform pan bottom if you use a small thin spatula dipped in cornstarch. After transferring each strip, wipe the spatula clean with paper toweling, then dip again in cornstarch. Lay 1 long strip right across the center of the wax-paper-covered pan bottom, then add 3 more strips to either side, spacing them about ¾ inch apart and making sure that you don't use up all of the long strips. Next, lay 7 strips at right angles to the first 7 strips, again spacing them ¾ inch apart. *Note: Don't worry if any of the strips break as you fashion the lattice top; simply pinch the broken ends back together. The mending will never show.* Using the springform pan bottom to support the lattice top, very carefully invert it over the filled pie shell and gently peel off the wax paper. Trim any overlong strips—the lattice should completely cover the cherry filling but not overhang the crimped edge. Moisten both ends of each strip with cool water and crimp them into the fluted pie edge to seal.

Slide the pie onto the baking sheet in the preheated oven and bake 10 minutes. Reduce the oven temperature to moderate (350° F.) and bake 40 to 45 minutes longer, until the pastry is nicely browned and the filling bubbly. *Note: Cover any portions of the fluted edge or lattice strips that threaten to over-brown with strips of foil.* Serve hot or at room temperature.

DRIED APRICOT PIE WITH SPICY PASTRY

MAKES 8 SERVINGS

PASTRY:

1¼ cups sifted cornstarch

¾ cup sifted all-purpose flour

2 tablespoons sugar

1 teaspoon butter flavor granules

½ teaspoon finely grated orange zest

½ teaspoon ground ginger

¼ teaspoon ground cardamom

¼ teaspoon ground cinnamon

¼ teaspoon freshly grated nutmeg

7 tablespoons extra-light olive oil or vegetable oil (canola, safflower, sunflower, corn oil, etc.)

6 tablespoons cold water

1 tablespoon liquid egg substitute

GLAZE:

2 tablespoons whole milk mixed with 2 teaspoons sugar

For the Pastry: Preheat the oven to moderately hot (375° F.). Mix the cornstarch, flour, sugar, butter granules, orange zest, ginger, cardamom, cinnamon, and nutmeg in a large shallow bowl. Whisk the oil with the water and egg substitute in a 2-cup measure until creamy. Drizzle over the cornstarch mixture, then fork briskly until crumbly. If not all of the dry ingredients are moistened, work the mixture *lightly* with your hands until uniformly crumbly. Gather the pastry into a ball, place on a 12-inch square of wax paper, then flatten with your hands into a thick round about 6 inches in diameter. Top with a second square of wax paper, set on a slightly dampened counter, then, with short, quick strokes, roll the pastry from the center outward into a 12-inch circle.

Carefully peel off the top piece of paper, center a 9-inch pie pan upside-down on the pastry, then, using the bottom sheet of wax paper for support, quickly but gently invert the pan and the pastry together—the pastry will ease into the pan. Now gently peel off the remaining sheet of wax paper and pat the pastry against the bottom and sides of the pan, making sure there are no holes. Trim the pastry overhang so that it is about 1 inch larger than the pie pan, then roll the edges under until they rest on the rim of the pan and crimp, making a fluted edge. Prick the bottom and sides of the crust well with the tines of a fork. *Note: It's not necessary to weight this pie shell before you bake it. It will not shrink the way a conventional crust does.*

Bake for 15 minutes in the lower two thirds of the preheated oven until pale tan and crisp, then cool on a wire rack for at least 30 minutes before filling. Meanwhile, gather the pastry trimmings into a ball and roll about ⅛ inch thick between 2 pieces of wax paper. Very carefully peel off the top piece of wax paper, place a baking sheet on top of the pastry, then, using the bottom sheet of wax

FILLING:

1 pound dried, pitted apricots

1 (12-ounce) can peach nectar

1 cinnamon stick, split lengthwise

1 cup water

⅓ cup sugar

1 tablespoon cornstarch

½ teaspoon ground cinnamon

2 tablespoons orange marmalade

1 tablespoon freshly squeezed lemon juice

PER SERVING: 444 C   4 g P   12.7 g TF
(1.8 g SAT)   84 g CARB   36 mg S
0.3 mg CH

paper for support, invert. Carefully peel off the top piece of wax paper and, using star, heart, crescent, or other fancy cutters measuring 1 to 2 inches across, make the cutouts right on the baking sheet and peel away the trimmings. Using a pastry brush, spread the glaze over the cutouts, taking care that it does not run down onto the baking sheet and "glue" the cutouts to the sheet. Bake 12 minutes in the middle of the preheated oven, then cool and reserve. Leave the oven set at 375° F.

Meanwhile, Prepare the Filling: Mix the apricots, peach nectar, cinnamon stick, and water in a heavy medium-size saucepan and bring to a boil over moderate heat. Adjust the heat so the mixture bubbles gently, then simmer, uncovered, 30 minutes. Remove from the heat, cover, and let stand 20 minutes. Discard the cinnamon stick. Combine the sugar, cornstarch, ground cinnamon, marmalade, and lemon juice with the apricot mixture and spoon into the pie shell.

Slide the pie onto a baking sheet and bake 25 minutes in the preheated oven until bubbly. Arrange the pastry cutouts decoratively on top of the filling and bake 5 minutes more. Serve hot or at room temperature.

ERINGUE-FROSTED APPLE CUSTARD TART

MAKES 8 SERVINGS

⚖

PASTRY:

1 recipe Low-Cholesterol Piecrust (page 64) or Vegetable Oil Pastry (page 66)

FILLING:

2 medium-size sweet apples such as Rome Beauties
1 tablespoon water
⅓ cup plus 1 tablespoon sugar
4 whole cloves
2 (1½- × ½-inch) strips lemon zest
½ cinnamon stick, split lengthwise
⅛ teaspoon ground ginger
½ cup whole milk
¼ cup plain lowfat yogurt
2 tablespoons Calvados, applejack, or brandy
1 tablespoon all-purpose flour
3 egg whites

MERINGUE:

3 egg whites
Pinch of salt
Pinch of cream of tartar
¼ cup confectioners' sugar

PER SERVING: 218 C 5 g P 6.2 g TF (1 g SAT) 37 g CARB 80 mg S 2.6 mg CH

Deceptively rich and creamy.

For the Pastry: Prepare and roll the piecrust as recipe directs and fit into a 9-inch pie plate, forming a high fluted edge; refrigerate.

For the Filling: Quarter, but do not peel or core the apples. Place in a heavy, medium-size saucepan along with the water, the 1 tablespoon sugar, the cloves, lemon zest, cinnamon stick, and ginger. Cover and cook over moderately low heat 20 to 25 minutes until the apples are mushy; remove and discard the cloves, lemon zest, and cinnamon stick. Put the apple mixture through a food mill, then cool the applesauce to room temperature and smooth it over the bottom of the pie shell.

Preheat the oven to hot (400° F.). Whisk together the milk, yogurt, Calvados, flour, egg whites, and the remaining ⅓ cup sugar. Pour slowly on top of the applesauce and bake the pie 15 minutes in the preheated oven. Reduce the oven temperature to moderately slow (325° F.), and bake 20 minutes longer, or just until the custard has set. Remove the pie from the oven and raise the oven temperature to moderate (350° F.).

For the Meringue: Beat the egg whites in the small electric mixer bowl at medium speed until foamy. Add the salt and cream of tartar and beat to soft peaks. Add the confectioners' sugar and beat until stiff and glossy. Spread the meringue on top of the pie, swirling it into peaks and valleys and making sure that it touches the piecrust all around. Bake 5 minutes longer, or just until the meringue is set and lightly browned. Let the pie cool to room temperature before serving.

CHOCOLATE SATIN TART

MAKES 8 SERVINGS

PASTRY:

1 recipe Low-Cholesterol Piecrust (page 64) or Vegetable Oil Pastry (page 66)

FILLING:

⅓ cup sugar

2 tablespoons unsweetened Dutch process cocoa powder

1 cup evaporated skim milk

Pinch of salt

3 egg whites

1 tablespoon cornstarch

½ teaspoon vanilla

1 tablespoon unsalted soft tub margarine (not extra-light)

1 recipe Mock Whipped Cream (page 174)

PER SERVING: 222 C   6 g P   8.4 g TF (1.6 g SAT)   31 g CARB   123 mg S   2.1 mg CH

For the Pastry: Prepare the piecrust as the recipe directs, roll and fit into a 9-inch tart tin that has a removable bottom, then bake fully, cool for 30 minutes, and reserve.

For the Filling: Blend 3 tablespoons of the sugar with the cocoa in a heavy medium-size saucepan, pressing out all lumps, then mix in ¾ cup of the milk and the salt. Warm over moderate heat until small bubbles appear around the edges of the pan. Meanwhile, whisk the egg whites with the remaining sugar and milk until frothy, then blend in the cornstarch. Gradually whisk a little of the hot mixture into the egg white mixture, then stir back into saucepan. Cook, stirring constantly, until thickened and smooth—about 2 minutes. *Note: Do not allow the mixture to boil or it will curdle.* Put through a fine sieve, then mix in the vanilla and margarine. Place a sheet of wax paper flat on the surface of the chocolate cream to prevent a skin from forming, cool to room temperature, then chill 1 to 2 hours.

Fold 2 cups of the Mock Whipped Cream into the chilled chocolate cream and spoon into the prepared pie shell. Scoop the remaining Mock Whipped Cream into a pastry bag fitted with a large star tip and decorate the top of the pie with a starburst pattern. Serve at once.

LEMON
ANGEL
PIE

MAKES 8 SERVINGS

FOR PREPARING THE PIE PAN:

1 teaspoon unsalted soft tub margarine
(not extra-light)

1 tablespoon all-purpose flour

MERINGUE PIE SHELL:

3 extra-large egg whites

⅛ teaspoon cream of tartar

1 cup superfine sugar

LEMON FILLING:

1 cup liquid egg substitute

½ cup granulated sugar

1 envelope unflavored gelatin

1 tablespoon unsalted soft tub margarine
(not extra-light)

¼ cup freshly squeezed lemon juice

1 tablespoon finely grated lemon zest

5 tablespoons superfine sugar

¼ cup boiling water

3 tablespoons meringue powder
(see page xviii)

This pie must chill for at least 4 hours, so allow yourself plenty of time.

*P*reheat the oven to very slow (275° F.). Grease a 9-inch pie pan well with the margarine, add the flour, then tilt the pan from side to side until evenly filmed with flour. Tap out any excess flour and set the pan aside.

For the Meringue Pie Shell: In an electric mixer (preferably one with a wire whip attachment), beat the egg whites and cream of tartar at moderately slow speed until frothy; then, with the mixer still running, add the sugar, 1 tablespoon at a time, pausing about 5 seconds between additions. When all of the sugar has been added, raise the mixer speed to high and beat the meringue about 5 minutes until very stiff and glossy. Using a tablespoon, smooth the meringue over the bottom and up the sides of the prepared pie pan, shaping it into a pie shell about 1 inch thick. Bake in the preheated oven for 1 hour until crisp and the palest of ivories, turn the oven off, and cool the meringue shell in the oven for about 2 hours or until room temperature.

Meanwhile, Prepare the Lemon Filling: Combine the egg substitute, granulated sugar, and gelatin in the top of a double boiler and let stand at room temperature 5 minutes. Set over simmering water and cook, stirring often, about 10 minutes, until the consistency of thin custard. Pour into a large heatproof bowl, add the margarine, and when it melts, stir in the lemon juice and zest. Set in an ice bath and chill 15 to 20 minutes, whisking often, until the mixture mounds softly when a bit of it is taken up on a metal spoon.

*D*issolve the superfine sugar in the boiling water in a medium-size heatproof bowl; add the me-

OPTIONAL GARNISHES:

1 recipe Mock Whipped Cream
(page 174)
1 twist of lemon
2 sprigs lemon geranium, lemon
verbena, or mint

PER SERVING: 231 C   6 g P   1.8 g TF   (0.3
g SAT)   49 g CARB   75 mg S   0 mg CH

ringue powder and beat with a hand electric beater at highest speed for 3 to 4 minutes, until as stiff and glossy as 7-minute icing. Stir about ½ cup of the meringue into the lemon mixture, then gently fold in the balance until no streaks of white or yellow show.

*P*our into the meringue shell, swirling the filling into hills and valleys; set, uncovered, in the refrigerator and chill at least 4 hours. Garnish, if you like, by piping rosettes of Mock Whipped Cream around the edge of the filling, standing a lemon twist in the center of the pie, and tucking a lemon geranium sprig on either side of it.

V A R I A T I O N S :

♣ *Orange Angel Pie* (8 servings): Prepare as directed, but in the filling, substitute orange zest for lemon zest and increase the amount to 4 teaspoons. Do not substitute orange juice for lemon juice.

PER SERVING: 231 C   6 g P   1.8 g TF   (0.3 g SAT)   50 g CARB   75 mg S   0 mg CH

♣ *Lime Angel Pie* (8 servings): Prepare as directed, but in the filling, substitute lime juice and zest for the lemon juice and zest.

PER SERVING: 231 C   6 g P   1.8 g TF   (0.3 g SAT)   49 g CARB   75 mg S   0 mg CH

CHOCOLATE ANGEL PIE

MAKES 8 SERVINGS

FOR PREPARING THE PIE PAN:

1 teaspoon unsalted soft tub margarine (not extra-light)

1 tablespoon all-purpose flour

MERINGUE PIE SHELL:

3 extra-large egg whites

⅛ teaspoon cream of tartar

1 cup superfine sugar

1 teaspoon vanilla

CHOCOLATE FILLING:

3½ teaspoons unflavored gelatin

2 tablespoons granulated sugar

3 tablespoons unsweetened Dutch process cocoa powder

2 cups evaporated skim milk

2 tablespoons unsalted soft tub margarine (not extra-light)

2 tablespoons coffee liqueur (optional)

1 teaspoon vanilla

5 tablespoons superfine sugar

¼ cup boiling water

3 tablespoons meringue powder (see page xviii)

PER SERVING: 252 C   8 g P   3.7 g TF   (0.8 g SAT)   47 g CARB   122 mg S   2.6 mg CH

The filling of this cloud-light pie needs about 8 hours in the refrigerator if it is to set properly.

Preheat the oven to very slow (275° F.). Grease a 9-inch pie pan well with the margarine, add the flour, then tilt the pan from side to side until evenly filmed with flour. Tap out any excess flour and set the pan aside.

For the Meringue Pie Shell: In an electric mixer (preferably one with a wire whip attachment), beat the egg whites and cream of tartar at moderately slow speed until frothy; then, with the mixer still running, add the sugar, 1 tablespoon at a time, pausing about 5 seconds between additions. When all of the sugar has been added, sprinkle in the vanilla, raise the mixer speed to high, and beat the meringue about 5 minutes until very stiff and glossy. Using a tablespoon, smooth the meringue over the bottom and up the sides of the prepared pie pan, shaping it into a pie shell about 1 inch thick. Bake in the preheated oven for 1 hour until crisp and pale ivory, turn the oven off, and cool the meringue shell in the oven for about 2 hours or until room temperature.

Meanwhile, Prepare the Chocolate Filling: Combine the gelatin, granulated sugar, and cocoa in a medium-size heavy saucepan, stir in the milk, and let stand 5 minutes. Set over moderately low heat and cook and stir 3 to 5 minutes until the gelatin dissolves completely. Add the margarine, reduce the heat to low, and cook and stir 2 to 3 minutes until the mixture is smooth. Remove from the heat and mix in the coffee liqueur, if you like, and the vanilla. Pour into a large heatproof bowl, set in an ice bath, and chill 20 to 25 minutes, whisking often, until the mixture mounds when you take a bit of it up on a spoon.

Dissolve the superfine sugar in the boiling water in a medium-size heatproof bowl; add the meringue powder and beat with a hand electric beater at highest speed for 3 to 4 minutes, until as stiff and glossy as 7-minute icing. Stir about ½ cup of the meringue into the chocolate mixture, then gently fold in the balance until no streaks of white or brown show.

Pour into the meringue shell, swirling the filling into hills and valleys; set, uncovered, in the refrigerator, and chill at least 8 hours or overnight before serving.

CHOCOLATE-HAZELNUT DACQUOISE

MAKES 16 SERVINGS

FOR PREPARING THE BAKING SHEETS:

1 tablespoon unsalted soft tub margarine (not extra-light)

2 tablespoons all-purpose flour

MERINGUE:

1½ cups skinned, toasted hazelnuts (see headnote)

1 cup plus 2 tablespoons sugar

⅓ cup sifted cornstarch

5 extra-large egg whites

¼ teaspoon cream of tartar

⅛ teaspoon salt

½ teaspoon vanilla

CHOCOLATE CREAM:

3 cups sugar

½ cup unsweetened Dutch process cocoa powder

1 cup evaporated skim milk

2 tablespoons light corn syrup

2 tablespoons unsalted soft tub margarine (not extra-light)

2 teaspoons vanilla

$\mathcal{M}$ost dacquoises are filled with a chocolate- and cream-laden ganâche. This one reduces the saturated fat and cholesterol counts to nearly nothing. For this recipe's meringue and topping you will need 2¼ cups of unblanched, shelled hazelnuts. To toast the hazelnuts: spread them in a baking pan and set, uncovered, in a preheated moderate oven (350° F.) for 30 to 35 minutes until the skins begin to crack and the nuts underneath are a rich amber color. Cool 10 minutes, bundle in a clean tea towel, and rub briskly to remove the skins. Don't worry about any recalcitrant bits of skin still clinging to the nuts. They will add color.

$\mathcal{P}$reheat the oven to very slow (275° F.). Grease 2 baking sheets well, using ¼ tablespoon margarine for each. Sift 1 tablespoon flour over each sheet, tilt first to one side, then another, until covered with a thin, even film of flour. Tap the excess flour from each baking sheet. Using an 8-inch round cake pan as a guide, draw a circle in the middle of each baking sheet; set the baking sheets aside.

$\mathcal{F}$or the Meringue: Churn the hazelnuts, ¾ cup of the sugar, and the cornstarch in a food processor 15 to 20 seconds, pulsing part of the time, until uniformly fine; reserve. In the large electric mixer bowl, beat the egg whites at slow speed until frothy. Add the cream of tartar, salt, and vanilla and beat at slow speed to soft peaks. Raise the mixer speed to medium and add the remaining sugar, 1 tablespoon at a time. Continue beating the meringue until stiff and glossy but not dry—2 to 3 minutes. Scatter ⅓ of the hazelnut mixture over the meringue and fold in gently but thoroughly. Repeat twice more until all the nut mixture is incorporated.

$\mathcal{S}$mooth ½ the meringue into an 8-inch circle in the middle of each prepared baking sheet, leveling

DECORATION:
───────
¾ cup skinned, toasted hazelnuts, finely
chopped

PER SERVING: 367 C   5 g P   12.6 g TF   (1.3
g SAT)   62 g CARB   79 mg S   0.6 mg CH

the top and edges as much as possible. Bake the meringues 1 to 1¼ hours in the preheated oven until crisp, tan, and dry, reversing the position of the baking sheets halfway through. Cool to room temperature.

For the Chocolate Cream: Churn the sugar and cocoa in a food processor about 30 seconds until absolutely smooth. Add the milk and corn syrup and churn 30 seconds longer. Pour into a very large heavy saucepan and insert a candy thermometer. Drop in the margarine, set over moderately low heat, and cook, uncovered, without stirring, until the thermometer reaches 234° F. (this will take about 30 minutes) or until a little of the chocolate mixture, dropped into a little cold water, *almost* forms a soft ball. Remove from the heat at once and cool, without stirring, until the candy thermometer registers 120° F. (this will also take about 30 minutes). Meanwhile draw a 9-inch circle on a piece of heavy cardboard, cut it out, then wrap the circle smoothly in aluminum foil. Set aside. Add the vanilla to the cooled chocolate mixture, then beat with a hand electric mixer at highest speed until the chocolate cream is a good spreading consistency (it will lose its gloss and the beaters will begin to leave tracks that do not disappear). You will now have to work fast lest the chocolate cream become too stiff to spread easily. *Note: If this should happen, simply beat in a little water or evaporated skim milk. If, on the other hand, the cream just never thickens enough to spread, beat in a little confectioners' sugar.*

To Assemble the Dacquoise: Very carefully loosen a meringue circle with a spatula and place it flat-side-down, on the foil-covered cardboard circle. Spread it with about ⅓ of the chocolate cream, smoothing to within ½ inch of the edge all around. Place the second meringue circle, flat-side-down, on top, then frost the top and sides smoothly with the remaining chocolate cream.

To Decorate the Dacquoise: Dip a spatula into hot water and quickly smooth the chocolate cream on the top and sides of the dacquoise. With your hands, pat the chopped hazelnuts smoothly into the frosting around the sides of the dacquoise, then scatter a tablespoon or so of the remaining nuts artfully on top. Or, you might scatter a few coarsely broken skinned and toasted hazelnuts on top instead of the finely chopped ones. Let the dacquoise stand several hours at room temperature before cutting, and use your sharpest knife to do the job.

CHOCOLATE PASTA WITH CHOCOLATE SAUCE

MAKES 4 SERVINGS

PASTA:

1½ cups unsifted all-purpose flour

4 tablespoons unsweetened Dutch process cocoa powder

6 tablespoons sugar

Pinch of salt

1 egg white

2 teaspoons corn oil

3 tablespoons water

CHOCOLATE SAUCE:

2 tablespoons all-purpose flour

1 teaspoon cornstarch

2 tablespoons unsweetened Dutch process cocoa powder

¼ cup superfine sugar

1 teaspoon instant espresso coffee crystals

1 cup evaporated skim milk

1 tablespoon honey

1 tablespoon unsalted soft tub margarine (not extra-light)

¾ teaspoon vanilla

OPTIONAL TOPPING:

1 cup Mock Whipped Cream (page 174)

PER SERVING: 447 C   12 g P   7.1 g TF   (1.8 g SAT)   86 g CARB   180 mg S   2.6 mg CH

Nowhere is it written that pasta must always be savory.

For the Pasta: Combine the flour, cocoa, sugar, and salt on a work surface and make a well in the center. Combine the egg white, oil, and water, pour into the well, then, using a fork, gradually pull the dry ingredients into the middle of the well until you have a soft workable dough. Knead the dough a few minutes, adding a little more flour if it seems sticky.

If you have a pasta machine, roll the dough out as the manufacturer directs to the next-to-the-thinnest thickness, then put through the cutters for making fettucine. If shaping by hand, roll the dough on a lightly floured board to a thickness of ⅛ inch, then cut into strips ½ inch wide. Let stand while you prepare the sauce.

For the Chocolate Sauce: Blend the flour, cornstarch, cocoa, sugar, and coffee crystals in a small heavy saucepan, pressing out all lumps. Mix in the milk and honey, set over moderate heat, and cook, stirring constantly, about 3 minutes, until thickened and smooth. Add the margarine, reduce the heat to moderately low, and cook and stir 2 to 3 minutes until the margarine is melted and the sauce satin-smooth. Remove from the heat and stir in the vanilla. Keep warm.

To Cook the Pasta: Cook the pasta in a large kettle of boiling water about 2 minutes until *al dente*. Drain well, then divide among 4 plates and top with the warm chocolate sauce. Drift each portion, if you like, with Mock Whipped Cream and serve.

CANNOLI

MAKES 8 SERVINGS

COOKIE SHELLS:

½ cup sifted all-purpose flour

½ cup sugar

2 tablespoons cornstarch

¾ teaspoon finely grated orange zest

½ teaspoon ground cinnamon

¼ teaspoon freshly grated nutmeg

3 tablespoons extra-light olive oil or vegetable oil (canola, safflower, sunflower, corn oil, etc.)

2 egg whites

2 teaspoons cold water

¾ teaspoon vanilla

1 tablespoon butter flavor granules

CREAM FILLING:

1½ teaspoons unflavored gelatin

1½ tablespoons cold water

2 cups lowfat (1 percent) cottage cheese

⅓ cup sugar

½ teaspoon vanilla

4 teaspoons coarsely chopped blanched pistachio nuts

2 tablespoons minced mixed candied fruits

*T*he trouble with this Sicilian sweet is that it's deep-fat fried, then filled with a rich pastry cream. Not exactly what the doctor ordered. This cholesterol-trimmed variation is baked, and its filling is made with cottage cheese that contains only 1 percent butterfat. To keep the cannoli crisp, fill the cookie shells at the very last minute.

*P*reheat the oven to hot (400° F.). Spray a cookie sheet with nonstick vegetable cooking spray and set aside.

For the Cookie Shells: Combine the flour, sugar, cornstarch, orange zest, cinnamon, and nutmeg in a large bowl and make a well in the center. Whisk the oil with the egg whites, water, vanilla, and butter granules in a 2-cup measure until uniformly creamy, then dump the mixture into the well in the dry ingredients and beat just enough to combine. Do not overbeat at this point or the cookie shells will be tough.

*B*ecause these cookies are so large and apt to spread, you can only bake two of them at a time. For each one, spoon a scant 2 tablespoons of batter onto the prepared cookie sheet and smooth it into a circle; leave 3 inches between cookies. Have ready 2 cannoli molds for shaping the cookies into tubes—in a pinch you can use wooden spoons or whisks with very thick handles. Bake the cookies 9 to 10 minutes in the preheated oven until set and lightly browned. Remove from the oven, lift at once from the cookie sheet, and shape into a fat "cigar" by bending around a cannoli mold, spoon, or whisk handle. Repeat with the remaining cookie on the second mold, spoon, or whisk handle. As soon as the cookies are cool and crisp, carefully slide them off the molds. Repeat until all cookies are baked and shaped; store airtight.

OPTIONAL TOPPING:

3 tablespoons confectioners' sugar (for
dusting)

PER CANNOLI: 235 C   9 g P
6.8 g TF   (1.2 g SAT)   34 g CARB
319 mg S   2.5 mg CH

For the Cream Filling: Soften the gelatin in the water in a small heatproof measuring cup; set in a pan of simmering water and heat until the gelatin dissolves completely; set aside to cool. Buzz the cottage cheese in a food processor until smooth, about 1 minute. Pulse in the sugar and vanilla, then the gelatin, and churn until blended. Transfer to a medium-size bowl and fold in the pistachios and candied fruits. Cover with plastic food wrap and refrigerate until slightly firm, about 1 hour. Spoon the filling into a pastry bag fitted with a large plain tip and refrigerate until ready to serve.

At serving time, pipe the filling into the cookie shells and, if you like, dust each liberally with confectioners' sugar.

4

CAKES, COFFEE CAKES, AND COOKIES

ANGEL ROLL WITH TART LEMON FILLING

MAKES 8 SERVINGS

LEMON FILLING:

3 tablespoons cornstarch
⅓ cup sugar
1 teaspoon finely grated lemon zest
⅓ cup freshly squeezed lemon juice
¾ cup water
1 tablespoon unsalted soft tub margarine
(not extra-light)

FOR PREPARING THE CAKE PAN:

Nonstick vegetable cooking spray
1½ teaspoons unsalted soft tub
margarine (not extra-light)
1 rounded tablespoon all-purpose flour

If this cake is to have the proper flavor, you must use freshly squeezed lemon juice. The bottled variety will impart a bitter taste.

Make the Lemon Filling First: Combine the cornstarch and sugar in a small heavy saucepan, then mix in the lemon zest and juice and water. Set over moderate heat and cook, stirring constantly, until the mixture boils and thickens—about 3 minutes. Remove from the heat and mix in the margarine. Cool to room temperature, stirring often to prevent a skin from forming on the surface of the filling, then cover and refrigerate until ready to use. *Note: If you like, you can make the filling as much as a day ahead of time. Let it come to room temperature before using, and stir to restore it to good spreading consistency.*

For Preparing the Cake Pan: Spray the bottom of a 15½ × 10½ × 1-inch jelly roll pan lightly with the nonstick spray, then smooth a cut-to-fit piece of baking parchment or wax paper over the bottom of the pan. Now grease the parchment and the pan sides evenly with the margarine, add the flour, and tilt the pan from side to side until the parchment and pan sides are evenly filmed with flour. Tap out the excess flour and set the pan aside.

For the Cake: Preheat the oven to slow (300° F.). Beat the egg whites with the cream of tartar and salt to very soft peaks. Sprinkle 2 tablespoons of the granulated sugar over the whites and fold in gently, using a rubber spatula or flat wire whisk. Continue folding the granulated sugar in, 2 tablespoons at a time, until all of it has been incorporated. Use the lightest touch possible at all times lest you knock the air out of the beaten whites. Now sift 2 tablespoons of the flour over the whites and fold in gently using a flat wire whisk. Continue folding in the balance of the flour the same way, 2 tablespoons at a time. Fold in the lemon juice, vanilla, and almond extract.

CAKE:

4 jumbo egg whites

⅛ teaspoon cream of tartar

⅛ teaspoon salt

½ cup sifted granulated sugar

½ cup sifted cake flour, sifted twice again

2 teaspoons freshly squeezed lemon juice

½ teaspoon vanilla

¼ teaspoon almond extract

3 tablespoons confectioners' sugar

OPTIONAL GARNISHES:

Twists of lemon

Sprigs of lemon verbena or lemon geranium

PER SERVING: 164 C   3 g P   2.3 g TF   (0.4 g SAT)   33 g CARB   70 mg S   0 mg CH

*P*our the batter into the prepared pan, smoothing it evenly into the corners. Bake about 25 minutes in the preheated oven until springy to the touch. The cake will be pale, but don't bake any longer or it will toughen. Meanwhile, spread a kitchen towel on the counter and sift the confectioners' sugar over it to cover an area approximately the size of the cake.

*T*he instant you take the cake from the oven, invert it on the sugared towel and peel off the parchment. Using a sharp serrated knife, trim off any crisp edges that might crack when the cake is rolled. With one of the short ends toward you, roll the cake up in the towel and let it cool 35 minutes.

*U*nroll the cake, spread it evenly with the lemon filling, leaving ½ inch margins all around, then re-roll, jelly-roll style, and let stand, covered with the towel, 20 minutes. Remove the towel and sift any loose confectioners' sugar over the cake. Ease the roll onto a platter and garnish, if you like, with lemon twists and sprigs of lemon verbena or lemon geranium.

CLOUD-HIGH ANGEL FOOD CAKE

MAKES A 10-INCH TUBE CAKE,
12 SERVINGS

1¾ cups egg whites (about 10 jumbo eggs)

¾ teaspoon cream of tartar

¼ teaspoon salt

1¾ cups sifted sugar

1¼ cups sifted cake flour, sifted twice again

2 teaspoons vanilla

½ teaspoon almond extract

½ teaspoon freshly squeezed lemon juice

OPTIONAL TOPPING:

4 cups lightly crushed fresh berries or thinly sliced peeled and pitted peaches, sweetened to taste

PER SERVING: 169 C   5 g P   0 g TF   (0 g SAT)   37 g CARB   104 mg S   0 mg CH

The secret of making fine and feathery angel food cakes is in baking them in a slow oven, also in beating the egg whites just until they billow and peak softly. Never, ever, whip them to stiff peaks.

Preheat the oven to slow (300° F.). Beat the egg whites with the cream of tartar and salt to very soft peaks. Sprinkle 2 tablespoons of the sugar over the whites and fold in gently, using a rubber spatula or flat wire whisk. Continue folding the sugar in, 2 tablespoons at a time, until all of it has been incorporated. Use the lightest touch possible at all times lest you knock the air out of the beaten whites. Now sift 2 tablespoons of the flour over the whites and fold in gently using a flat wire whisk. Continue folding in the balance of the flour the same way, 2 tablespoons at a time. Fold in the vanilla, almond extract, and lemon juice.

Pour the batter into an ungreased 10-inch tube pan and smooth the surface lightly with a rubber spatula. Rap the pan once or twice against the counter to release large air bubbles, then bake the cake 1 hour and 10 minutes in the preheated oven until pale brown and springy to the touch. Remove the cake from the oven, invert at once, and let stand upside-down on the counter for 1 hour. Turn the cake right-side-up, loosen around the edges and also around the central tube, then invert on a cake plate. To cut, use a sharp serrated knife and a seesaw motion or a piece of fine thread, taking care not to compact the cake. Serve as is or top with the lightly crushed fresh berries or sliced peaches.

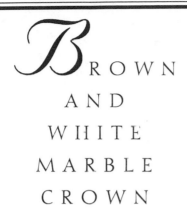

BROWN AND WHITE MARBLE CROWN

MAKES A 10-INCH BUNDT CAKE,
12 SERVINGS

FOR PREPARING THE PAN:

1 tablespoon unsalted soft tub margarine
(not extra-light)

2 tablespoons sugar

CAKE:

1¼ cups egg whites (about 8 jumbo
eggs)

½ teaspoon cream of tartar

¼ teaspoon salt

1½ teaspoons vanilla

1½ cups sifted sugar

¾ cup sifted cake flour, sifted twice
again and divided into 2 equal parts

3 tablespoons sifted unsweetened Dutch
process cocoa powder

PER SERVING: 152 C   3 g P   1.2 g TF   (0.3
g SAT)   33 g CARB   96 mg S   0 mg CH

*P*reheat the oven to slow (300° F.). Carefully grease a 10-inch (12-cup) Bundt pan with the margarine, add the 2 tablespoons sugar, and tilt the pan first to one side, then to the other, until all surfaces are evenly coated with sugar. Tap out any excess sugar and set the pan aside.

For the Cake: Beat the egg whites with the cream of tartar, salt, and vanilla to very soft peaks. Sprinkle 2 tablespoons of the sugar over the whites and fold in gently, using a rubber spatula or flat wire whisk. Continue folding the sugar in, 2 tablespoons at a time, until all of it has been incorporated. Use the lightest touch possible lest you knock the air out of the beaten whites.

*Q*uickly divide the egg white mixture in half, putting them into separate bowls; also sift half the flour with the cocoa onto a piece of wax paper. Sift the cocoa mixture, 1 tablespoon at a time, over half the beaten whites, folding it in gently but thoroughly after each addition. Now sift the other half of the flour, 1 tablespoon at a time, over the remaining beaten whites, and fold it in gently but thoroughly. Pour the chocolate batter on top of the white batter and, very gently, fold in just enough to create a marbleized effect. Pour the batter into the prepared pan and smooth the surface with a rubber spatula. Rap the pan once or twice against the counter to release large air bubbles.

*B*ake the cake 1 hour in the preheated oven until lightly browned and springy to the touch. Remove the cake from the oven, invert at once onto a cake plate, and let stand upside-down for 1 hour. If the cake does not drop out during this cooling period, loosen carefully around the edges and central tube, then invert on the plate. To cut, use a sharp serrated knife and a seesaw motion or a piece of fine thread, taking care not to compact the cake.

ANGEL SAVARINS WITH SLICED PEACHES IN CRIMSON SAUCE

MAKES 8 SERVINGS

FOR PREPARING THE
SAVARIN MOLDS:

_2 tablespoons unsalted soft tub
margarine (not extra-light)_

3 tablespoons sugar

CAKE:

_¾ cup egg whites (about 5 extra-large
eggs)_

½ teaspoon cream of tartar

¼ teaspoon salt

¾ cup sifted sugar

_½ cup sifted cake flour, sifted twice
again_

1 teaspoon Grand Marnier

1 teaspoon freshly squeezed lemon juice

½ teaspoon almond extract

Preheat the oven to slow (300° F.). Lightly grease 8 savarin or individual ring molds with the margarine, then spoon a little of the sugar into each one, and tilt until evenly coated with sugar; tap the excess sugar out of each mold and set the molds aside.

For the Cake: Beat the egg whites with the cream of tartar and salt to very soft peaks. Sprinkle 2 tablespoons of the sugar over the whites and fold in gently, using a rubber spatula or flat wire whisk. Continue folding the sugar in, 2 tablespoons at a time, until all of it has been incorporated. Use the lightest touch possible at all times lest you knock the air out of the beaten whites. Now sift 2 tablespoons of the flour over the whites and fold in gently using a flat wire whisk. Continue folding in the balance of the flour the same way, 2 tablespoons at a time. Fold in the Grand Marnier, lemon juice, and almond extract. Spoon the batter into the prepared savarin molds, filling each no more than ⅔ full.

Rap each mold sharply against the counter once or twice to expel large air bubbles, then arrange, not touching, on a baking sheet, and bake 30 to 35 minutes in the preheated oven until pale tan and springy to the touch. Invert the molds at once on a wire rack and cool 5 minutes. Gently loosen the cakes from their molds using a small thin-bladed spatula or paring knife, turn out on the rack, and cool to room temperature.

Meanwhile, Prepare the Peaches in Crimson Sauce: Blanch the peaches 30 seconds in boiling water, drain, peel, pit and slice ¼ inch thick. Place the peaches in a large bowl, add the lemon juice, and toss well to mix. Churn the raspberries, sugar, and Grand Marnier in a food processor 60 seconds until smooth. Press through a fine sieve to remove

PEACHES IN CRIMSON SAUCE:

---

4 large ripe peaches
1 tablespoon freshly squeezed lemon juice
1 pint raspberries
⅓ cup superfine sugar
1 tablespoon Grand Marnier

<u>PER SERVING</u>: 241 C   4 g P   3 g TF   (0.5 g SAT)   50 g CARB   112 mg S   0 mg CH

the raspberry seeds, pour the purée over the peaches, and toss well to mix.

To serve, fill the center of each savarin with some of the Peaches in Crimson Sauce and pass the rest in a sauceboat.

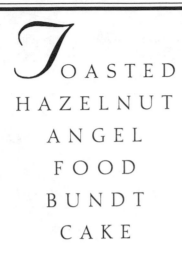

TOASTED HAZELNUT ANGEL FOOD BUNDT CAKE

MAKES A 10-INCH BUNDT CAKE,
12 SERVINGS

FOR PREPARING THE PAN:

1 tablespoon unsalted soft tub margarine
(not extra-light)
2 tablespoons sugar

CAKE:

¾ cup skinned, toasted, shelled
hazelnuts (see headnote, page 92)
1 cup sifted cake flour, sifted twice again
1¼ cups egg whites (about 8 jumbo
eggs)
½ teaspoon cream of tartar
¼ teaspoon salt
1½ cups sifted sugar
1½ teaspoons vanilla

PER SERVING: 203 C   5 g P   5.5 g TF   (0.5
g SAT)   35 g CARB   92 mg S   0 mg CH

*P*reheat the oven to slow (300° F.). Carefully grease a 10-inch (12-cup) Bundt pan with the margarine, add the 2 tablespoons sugar, and tilt the pan first to one side, then to the other, until all surfaces are evenly coated with sugar. Tap out any excess sugar and set the pan aside.

For the Cake: Pulse the nuts in a food processor 1 to 2 minutes until very finely ground but not pasty. Combine ⅓ cup of the sifted flour with the ground nuts and set aside.

*B*eat the egg whites with the cream of tartar and salt to very soft peaks. Sprinkle 2 tablespoons of the sugar over the whites and fold in gently, using a rubber spatula or flat wire whisk. Continue folding the sugar in, 2 tablespoons at a time, until all of it has been incorporated. Use the lightest touch possible at all times lest you knock the air out of the beaten whites. Now sift 2 tablespoons of the remaining ⅔ cup flour over the whites and fold in gently using a flat wire whisk. Continue folding in the balance of the flour the same way, 2 tablespoons at a time. Fold in the vanilla, add the hazelnut-flour mixture all at once, and fold it in lightly but thoroughly. Pour the batter into the prepared pan and smooth the surface with a rubber spatula. Rap the pan once or twice against the counter to release large air bubbles.

*B*ake the cake 1 hour in the preheated oven until lightly browned and springy to the touch. Remove the cake from oven, invert at once onto a cake plate, and let stand upside-down for 1 hour. If the cake does not drop out during this cooling period, loosen carefully around the edges and central tube, then invert on the plate. To cut, use a sharp serrated knife and a seesaw motion or a piece of fine thread, taking care not to compact the cake.

SPICY ZUCCHINI CAKE

MAKES 18 SERVINGS

2¼ cups sifted all-purpose flour
¾ teaspoon baking powder
¾ teaspoon baking soda
¾ teaspoon ground cinnamon
½ teaspoon ground ginger
¼ teaspoon freshly grated nutmeg
¼ teaspoon ground allspice
1 cup sugar
⅓ cup seedless raisins
⅓ cup coarsely chopped pecans
½ cup liquid egg substitute
½ cup extra-light olive oil or vegetable oil (canola, safflower, sunflower, corn oil, etc.)
1 teaspoon vanilla
½ cup well-drained canned crushed pineapple
1½ cups moderately finely chopped zucchini (measure loosely packed)
1 tablespoon freshly squeezed lemon juice

<u>PER SERVING</u>: 180 C   2 g P   7.8 g TF (1 g SAT)   26 g CARB   62 mg S   0 mg CH

The quickest way to chop the zucchini is in a food processor fitted with the metal chopping blade, but pulse carefully so that you don't reduce the squash to mush. If wrapped airtight, this tender-crumbed cake remains unbelievably moist for a week or more.

*P*reheat the oven to moderately slow (325° F.). Spray a 9 × 5 × 3-inch loaf pan with nonstick vegetable cooking spray and set aside. Sift the flour, baking powder, soda, cinnamon, ginger, nutmeg, allspice, and sugar into a large mixing bowl. Add the raisins and pecans and toss well to dredge, then make a well in the center of the dry ingredients. In a 1-quart measuring cup, mix the egg substitute with the oil, vanilla, pineapple, zucchini, and lemon juice, pour into the well in the dry ingredients, and stir just enough to mix. The batter will be thick and lumpy, but do not mix any further at this point or the cake may be tough. Spoon the batter into the prepared pan, spreading it well into the corners and smoothing the top.

*B*ake in the preheated oven for 1 to 1¼ hours, or until the cake is springy to the touch and a toothpick inserted in the center comes out clean. Cool 10 minutes on a wire rack in the upright pan, then invert the cake on the rack, turn right-side-up, and cool to room temperature. Slice ½ inch thick.

FRESH PEACH TORTE

MAKES A 9-INCH ROUND TORTE,
12 SERVINGS

PEACH TOPPING:

3 medium-size ripe peaches

1 tablespoon freshly squeezed lemon
juice

1 tablespoon granulated sugar mixed
with ¼ teaspoon ground cinnamon

TORTE:

1 cup sifted all-purpose flour

⅓ cup firmly packed light brown sugar

7 tablespoons granulated sugar

½ teaspoon baking powder

¾ teaspoon ground ginger

½ ground cinnamon

¼ teaspoon freshly grated nutmeg

⅛ teaspoon salt

½ cup extra-light olive oil or vegetable
oil (canola, safflower, sunflower, corn oil,
etc.)

⅓ cup liquid egg substitute

¼ cup skim milk

1 teaspoon butter flavor extract

1 teaspoon vanilla

3 egg whites

Make this dense, moist, French-style torte in summer when peaches are at their peak of flavor. If ripe peaches are unavailable, use nectarines.

Preheat the oven to moderately hot (375° F.); lightly spray a 9-inch round cake pan with non-stick vegetable cooking spray, line the bottom with wax paper, spray, then dust with flour and set aside.

For the Topping: Blanch the peaches 30 seconds in boiling water, drain, peel, pit, and slice ⅛ inch thick. Place the peaches in a bowl, add the lemon juice, and toss lightly to coat; set aside while you prepare the torte.

For the Torte: Combine the flour, brown sugar, 4 tablespoons of the granulatd sugar, the baking powder, ginger, cinnamon, nutmeg, and salt in a large mixing bowl, press out all lumps, and make a well in the center. In a small bowl, whisk the oil with the egg substitute, milk, butter extract, and vanilla until well blended. Dump into the well in the dry ingredients and stir just enough to combine. Don't overmix or the torte will be tough.

Beat the egg whites until soft peaks form. Gradually beat in the remaining 3 tablespoons granulated sugar and continue beating until stiff but not dry. Gently fold ¼ of the beaten whites into the batter, then fold in the balance. Pour the batter into the prepared pan.

Drain the peach slices well and arrange on top of the batter in a decorative design. Sprinkle evenly with the cinnamon-sugar. Bake in the preheated oven 1 hour or until the torte begins to pull away from the sides of the pan and is springy to the touch. Cool the torte upright in its pan on a wire rack 15 minutes (it will shrink somewhat, fall

GLAZE:

3 tablespoons red currant jelly

OPTIONAL
ACCOMPANIMENT:

Mock Whipped Cream (page 174)

PER SERVING: 204 C   3 g P   9.5 g TF   (1.4
g SAT)   28 g CARB   69 mg S   0.1 mg CH

slightly, too, but this is normal), then invert onto a wire rack, peel off the wax paper, and invert again so that the torte is right-side-up.

For the Glaze: Melt the jelly in a small heavy saucepan over low heat, then spread over the top of the torte. Serve the torte at room temperature, and accompany, if you like, with Mock Whipped Cream.

SPICY APPLE-PECAN CAKE

MAKES A 10-INCH BUNDT CAKE,
16 SERVINGS

FOR PREPARING THE PAN:

Nonstick vegetable cooking spray
2 tablespoons all-purpose flour

CAKE:

½ cup pecan halves
3 cups unsifted cake flour
1 teaspoon baking powder
½ teaspoon baking soda
½ teaspoon ground cinnamon
¼ teaspoon freshly grated nutmeg
¼ teaspoon ground allspice
⅛ teaspoon ground cloves
¼ teaspoon salt
1 cup extra-light olive oil or vegetable oil
(canola, safflower, sunflower, corn oil,
etc.)
2 tablespoons walnut oil
1 cup granulated sugar
½ cup firmly packed light brown sugar
1 cup liquid egg substitute
1 teaspoon vanilla

*P*reheat the oven to moderate (350° F.). Spray a 10-inch (12-cup) Bundt pan with the cooking spray, add the 2 tablespoons flour, and tilt the pan first to one side, then to another, until all surfaces are evenly coated with flour. Tap out any excess flour and set the pan aside.

For the Cake: Place the pecans in a pie tin and toast in the preheated oven until fragrant, about 7 minutes. Cool the nuts, coarsely chop, and reserve. Sift the flour with the baking powder, soda, cinnamon, nutmeg, allspice, cloves, and salt onto a piece of wax paper and set aside. Combine the olive and walnut oils and the granulated and brown sugars in the large bowl of an electric mixer and beat at medium speed until creamy. Gradually beat in the egg substitute, then add the vanilla. Remove from the mixer, fold in the sifted dry ingredients, then the apples, raisins, and reserved pecans. Spoon the batter into the prepared pan.

*B*ake in the preheated over for 50 minutes, or until a toothpick inserted in the center of the cake comes out clean. Cool the cake upright in its pan on a wire rack for 20 minutes, then loosen around the edge and central tube and invert on the rack. Cool the cake to room temperature, then dust with the confectioners' sugar.

3 cups peeled, cored, and thickly sliced apples (Northern Spy, Cortland, or Rome Beauty are best) tossed with 1 tablespoon freshly squeezed lemon juice (you'll need about 1¼ pounds apples)

1 cup golden seedless raisins (sultanas)

TOPPING:

3 tablespoons confectioners' sugar (for dusting)

PER SERVING: 361 C   4 g P   17.7 g TF   (2.2 g SAT)   49 g CARB   110 mg S   0 mg CH

Apple Upside-Down Cake

MAKES A 9-INCH ROUND CAKE, ABOUT 12 SERVINGS

APPLE MIXTURE:

1 tablespoon unsalted soft tub margarine (not extra-light)

1 tablespoon extra-light olive oil or vegetable oil (canola, safflower, sunflower, corn oil, etc.)

4 medium-size apples, peeled, cored, and cut into eighths

3 tablespoons firmly packed dark brown sugar

2 tablespoons freshly squeezed lemon juice

1½ tablespoons Calvados or apple brandy

CAKE:

1½ cups sifted all-purpose flour

⅔ cup sugar

1½ teaspoons baking powder

⅔ cup evaporated skim milk

¼ cup extra-light olive oil or vegetable oil (canola, safflower, sunflower, corn oil, etc.)

⅓ cup liquid egg substitute

*T*he best apples to use for this cake are Rome Beauties because they hold their shape so nicely, but you can also use Golden Delicious.

*P*reheat the oven to moderate (350° F.). Spray a 9-inch round layer cake pan with nonstick vegetable cooking spray and set aside.

For the Apple Mixture: Heat the margarine and oil in a large heavy skillet over moderate heat for 1 minute. Add the apples, tossing to coat. Add the brown sugar and lemon juice and cook, uncovered, shaking the pan occasionally, until the apples are almost tender—8 to 10 minutes. Add the Calvados and cook, uncovered, 3 minutes longer. Cool to room temperature, then arrange the apples in the bottom of the prepared pan in concentric rings; spoon any pan juices over the apples.

For the Cake: Combine the flour, sugar, and baking powder in a large mixing bowl and make a well in the center. In a large measuring cup whisk the milk with the oil, egg substitute, butter granules, vanilla, lemon zest, and almond extract until creamy and pour into the well in the dry ingredients. Stir just enough to mix—the batter will be quite thick and lumpy, but don't overmix at this point or the cake will be tough. Smooth the batter over the apples.

4 teaspoons butter flavor granules
1 teaspoon vanilla
1 teaspoon finely grated lemon zest
½ teaspoon almond extract

OPTIONAL TOPPING:

*Mock Whipped Cream (page 174) or
Labna (page 176)*

PER SERVING: 217 C   3 g P   7.1 g TF   (1 g
SAT)   35 g CARB   137 mg S   0.8 mg CH

*B*ake 30 to 35 minutes in the preheated oven, or until a cake tester inserted in the center of the cake comes out clean. Cool the cake upright in its pan on a wire rack for 10 minutes, then invert the cake on a serving plate. Carefully lift off the pan; if any apple slices have stuck to it, simply fit them back into place on the cake. Cut into wedges and serve warm or at room temperature. Top, if you like, with Mock Whipped Cream or Labna.

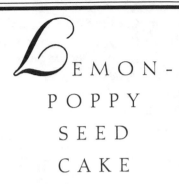

LEMON-POPPY SEED CAKE

MAKES A 9-INCH BUNDT CAKE,
ABOUT 16 SERVINGS

CAKE:

⅓ cup poppy seeds (make sure they are
good and fresh)

1½ cups sugar

2½ cups sifted all-purpose flour

1½ teaspons baking powder

½ teaspoon baking soda

⅛ teaspoon salt

1¼ teaspoons finely grated lemon zest

⅓ cup extra-light olive oil or vegetable
oil (canola, safflower, sunflower, corn oil,
etc.)

1 cup evaporated skim milk

¼ cup freshly squeezed lemon juice

1 tablespoon dry sherry

3 egg whites

This unusual cake is a little bit sweet, a little bit tart, but blessed most of all with a rich "nutty" flavor.

Preheat the oven to moderate (350° F.). Spray a 9-inch (8-cup) Bundt pan with nonstick vegetable cooking spray, lightly dust with flour, and set aside.

For the Cake: Place the poppy seeds in a pie tin and toast in the preheated oven 5 to 7 minutes until fragrant; cool and reserve.

Measure out 3 tablespoons of the sugar and reserve it for beating with the egg whites. Combine the remaining sugar, the flour, baking powder, soda, salt, and lemon zest in a large mixing bowl and make a well in the center. In a large measuring cup, whisk the oil with the milk, lemon juice, and sherry until creamy; set aside. Quickly beat the egg whites until foamy, then add the reserved 3 tablespoons sugar gradually, beating all the while, until the mixture peaks softly.

Dump the oil mixture into the well in the dry ingredients and stir just enough to combine. Do not overmix or the cake will be tough. Now fold in about ¼ of the beaten whites to lighten the batter. Finally, fold in the balance of the egg whites, then the toasted poppy seeds. Spoon the batter into the prepared pan and level the top.

Bake 50 minutes in the lower third of the preheated oven, or until a cake tester inserted near the center comes out clean. Cool the cake upright in its pan on a wire rack for 20 minutes, then loosen around the edge and central tube and invert on a cake plate.

For the Lemon Syrup: Combine the sugar and water in a small heavy saucepan, set over moderate heat, and cook 2 to 3 minutes until syrupy; stir in the lemon juice. Poke small holes into the top and sides of the cake using a toothpick or cake tester. Slowly spoon a little of the syrup over the cake, allowing it to sink in before adding more syrup. Cool the cake to room temperature, then let stand 1 hour before cutting.

LEMON SYRUP:

3 tablespoons sugar
1½ tablespoons water
3 tablespoons freshly squeezed lemon
juice

PER SERVING: 221 C   4 g P   6.2 g TF
(0.8 g SAT)   38 g CARB   113 mg S
0.6 mg CH

ZERO-CHOLESTEROL GRAPEFRUIT CAKE

MAKES AN 8½ × 4½ × 2½-INCH
LOAF CAKE, 12 SERVINGS

1½ cups sifted all-purpose flour
1 cup sugar
2 teaspoons baking powder
1 teaspoon ground ginger
¼ teaspoon ground mace
½ cup extra-light olive oil or vegetable
oil (canola, safflower, sunflower, corn oil,
etc.)
½ cup freshly squeezed grapefruit juice
4 teaspoons finely grated grapefruit zest
4 egg whites

PER SERVING: 208 C   3 g P   9.6 g TF   (1.4
g SAT)   29 g CARB   90 mg S   0 mg CH

*P*reheat the oven to moderate (350° F.). Liberally spray an 8½ × 4½ × 2½-inch loaf pan with non-stick vegetable cooking spray and set aside.

*S*ift the flour, ¾ cup of the sugar, the baking powder, ginger, and mace into a large mixing bowl and make a well in the center. In a large measuring cup, whisk the oil with the grapefruit juice and zest until uniformly creamy. Quickly beat the egg whites until foamy, gradually beat in the remaining ¼ cup sugar, and continue beating to soft peaks. Dump the oil mixture into the well in the dry ingredients and stir just enough to mix. The batter will be quite stiff and lumpy but do not beat any more at this point or the cake will be tough. Fold about ¼ of the beaten whites into the batter to lighten it, then fold in the balance until no streaks of white or yellow remain. Pour into the prepared pan.

*B*ake 45 to 50 minutes in the preheated oven until the cake is springy to the touch. Cool 10 minutes on a wire rack in the upright pan, then invert the cake on the rack, turn right-side-up, and cool to room temperature. Slice ½ inch thick.

CITRUS
CAKE

MAKES A 6-INCH FLUTED CAKE,
8 SERVINGS

FOR PREPARING THE PAN:

Nonstick vegetable cooking spray
2 tablespoons all-purpose flour

CAKE:

1¾ cups sifted all-purpose flour
¾ cup sugar
1 teaspoon baking powder
¼ teaspoon baking soda
⅛ teaspoon salt
⅛ teaspoon ground cloves
⅓ cup extra-light olive oil or vegetable oil (canola, safflower, sunflower, corn oil, etc.)
¾ cup freshly squeezed orange juice
1 tablespoon freshly squeezed lemon juice
1 tablespoon freshly squeezed lime juice
2 teaspoons finely grated orange zest
½ teaspoon finely grated lemon zest
½ teaspoon finely grated lime zest
4 egg whites

OPTIONAL TOPPING:

1 tablespoon confectioners' sugar (for dusting)

PER SERVING: 276 C   5 g P   9.7 g TF   (1.4 g SAT)   43 g CARB   142 mg S   0 mg CH

Preheat the oven to moderate (350° F.). Spray a 6-inch (8-cup), deep, fluted tube pan (I use a steamed pudding mold) with the cooking spray, add the 2 tablespoons flour, and tilt the pan first to one side, then to another, until all surfaces are evenly coated with flour. Tap out any excess flour and set the pan aside.

For the Cake: Sift the flour, ½ cup of the sugar, the baking powder, soda, salt, and cloves into a large mixing bowl and make a well in the center. In a large measuring cup, whisk the oil with the orange, lemon, and lime juices and the orange, lemon, and lime zests until uniformly creamy. Beat the egg whites until foamy, then add the remaining ¼ cup sugar gradually, and continue beating to soft peaks. Dump the oil mixture into the well in the dry ingredients and stir just enough to mix—the batter will be quite stiff and lumpy, but if you over-beat at this point the cake will be tough. Fold about ¼ of the beaten whites into the batter to lighten it, then fold in the balance until no streaks of white or yellow show. Spoon the batter into the prepared pan.

Bake in the preheated oven about 1 hour, or until a toothpick inserted near the center comes out clean. Cool the cake upright in its pan on a wire rack for 20 minutes, then invert on the rack, and cool to room temperature. Just before serving, dust, if you like, with confectioners' sugar.

FRESH GINGER CAKE WITH ORANGE

MAKES A 13 × 9 × 2-INCH LOAF, 24
(3 × 1⅝-INCH) BARS

3½ cups sifted all-purpose flour

1½ cups sugar

1 teaspoon baking soda

1 teaspoon ground cinnamon

½ teaspoon freshly grated nutmeg

⅛ teaspoon ground cloves

1 cup evaporated skim milk

1 cup molasses

¾ cup extra-light olive oil or vegetable
oil (canola, safflower, sunflower, corn oil,
etc.)

¾ cup liquid egg substitute

1 tablespoon cider vinegar

½ cup finely minced fresh ginger

Finely grated zest of 2 oranges

OPTIONAL TOPPING:

Mock Whipped Cream (page 174)

PER BAR: 219 C   3 g P   7.2 g TF   (1 g
SAT)   36 g CARB   59 mg S   0.4 mg CH

Unlike most gingerbreads, this one is made with finely minced fresh ginger, and that accounts for its unusual bite and moistness.

Preheat the oven to moderate (350° F.). Lightly spray a 13 × 9 × 2-inch baking pan with nonstick vegetable cooking spray and set aside.

Sift the flour, sugar, soda, cinnamon, nutmeg, and cloves together into a large mixing bowl and make a well in the center. In a 1-quart measuring cup, whisk the milk with the molasses, oil, egg substitute, and vinegar until uniformly creamy. Add the ginger and orange zest and whisk well again. Pour all at once into the well in the dry ingredients and stir just enough to mix—it's better for the batter to be slightly lumpy than to overbeat because the cake will then be tough.

Pour the batter into the prepared pan and spread evenly into the corners. Bake 40 to 45 minutes in the preheated oven until the cake is lightly browned and springy to the touch. Cool the cake upright in its pan on a wire rack to room temperature, then cut into 24 bars (approximately 3 × 1⅝ inches—2 cuts lengthwise and 7 crosswise). Serve either plain or topped with Mock Whipped Cream.

BLOND GINGERBREAD WITH FRESH BLUEBERRIES

MAKES A 9 × 9 × 2-INCH LOAF, 16
(2¼-INCH) SQUARES

2 cups sifted all-purpose flour
1 cup sugar
1 teaspoon baking soda
1 teaspoon ground cinnamon
¾ teaspoon ground ginger
½ teaspoon freshly grated nutmeg
1 cup lowfat buttermilk
*⅓ cup extra-light olive oil or vegetable
oil (canola, safflower, sunflower, corn oil,
etc.)*
¼ cup liquid egg substitute
3 tablespoons molasses
*1 cup fresh blueberries, stemmed and
patted dry on paper toweling*

TOPPING:

1 tablespoon sugar
¼ teaspoon ground cinnamon
⅛ teaspoon ground mace

PER SQUARE: 167 C   2 g P   4.9 g TF (0.8 g
SAT)   29 g CARB   74 mg S   0.6 mg CH

An unusually delicate gingerbread strewn with fresh blueberries. If you must use the frozen, thaw them, drain well, then pat very dry on paper toweling.

Preheat the oven to moderate (350° F.). Liberally spray a 9 × 9 × 2-inch baking pan with nonstick vegetable cooking spray and set aside.

Sift the flour, sugar, soda, cinnamon, ginger, and nutmeg together into a large mixing bowl and make a well in the center. In a 1-quart measuring cup, whisk the buttermilk with the oil, egg substitute, and molasses until uniformly creamy, pour into the well in the dry ingredients, and stir just enough to mix—it's better for the batter to be a bit lumpy than to overmix because the gingerbread will be tough. Fold in the blueberries, spoon the batter into the prepared pan, smooth well into the corners, and level the surface. Combine all topping ingredients and sprinkle evenly over the batter.

Bake the gingerbread about 45 minutes in the preheated oven, or until it begins to pull from the sides of the pan and is springy to the touch in the middle. Cool the gingerbread upright in its pan on a wire rack to room temperature, then cut into 16 (2¼-inch) squares and serve.

LTRAMOIST CARROT CAKE WITH ORANGE GLAZE

MAKES 18 SERVINGS

⚖

CAKE:

1½ cups sifted all-purpose flour

1½ teaspoons baking powder

¾ teaspoon baking soda

¾ teaspoon ground cinnamon

¼ teaspoon ground allspice

¾ cup granulated sugar

¼ cup firmly packed dark brown sugar

½ cup moderately coarsely chopped pecans or walnuts

¾ cup liquid egg substitute

½ cup extra-light olive oil or vegetable oil (canola, safflower, sunflower, corn oil, etc.)

2 teaspoons finely grated orange zest

1 teaspoon vanilla

1½ cups finely chopped carrots (measure loosely packed)

¾ cup canned crushed pineapple, with its liquid

To make short shrift of chopping the carrots, use a food processor fitted with the metal chopping blade.

For the Cake: Preheat the oven to moderate (350° F.). Spray a 9 × 5 × 3-inch loaf pan with nonstick vegetable cooking spray and set aside. Sift the flour, baking powder, soda, cinnamon, allspice, and granulated sugar into a large mixing bowl. Add the brown sugar and, using your fingers, press out all lumps. Add the pecans and toss well to dredge. In a 1-quart measuring cup, mix the egg substitute with the oil, orange zest, vanilla, carrots, and pineapple; pour into the well in the dry ingredients and stir just enough to mix. The batter will be thin and lumpy, but do not mix any further at this point or the cake may be tough. Pour the batter into the prepared pan, spreading it well into the corners and smoothing the top.

Bake in the preheated oven for 1 to 1¼ hours, or until the cake is springy to the touch and a toothpick inserted in the center comes out clean. Cool 10 minutes on a wire rack in the upright pan, then invert the cake on the rack, turn right-side-up, and cool to room temperature.

For the Glaze: Combine all ingredients in a small bowl and spread over the top of the cooled cake, letting the excess run down the sides. *Note: To avoid messy cleanup, set the cake rack on a counter covered with wax paper before glazing the cake.* Let the glaze harden several hours before cutting the cake. Slice ½ inch thick.

ORANGE GLAZE:

1 cup sifted confectioners' sugar
½ teaspoon finely grated orange zest
1 tablespoon freshly squeezed lemon
juice
¼ teaspoon water

<u>PER SERVING</u>: 190 C   2 g P   8.4 g TF (1 g
SAT)   28 g CARB   88 mg S   0 mg CH

CARROT-GINGER CAKE WITH LEMON GLAZE

MAKES A 9-INCH ROUND CAKE, 10 TO 12 SERVINGS

⚖

FOR PREPARING THE PAN:

Nonstick vegetable cooking spray
2 tablespoons all-purpose flour

CAKE:

1¼ cups sifted cake flour
1 teaspoon baking soda
¼ teaspoon ground cardamom
⅛ teaspoon ground cinnamon
¼ teaspoon salt
⅔ cup sugar
⅓ cup extra-light olive oil or vegetable oil (canola, safflower, sunflower, corn oil, etc.)
4 egg whites
1½ cups moderately finely shredded carrots
¼ cup moderately finely chopped unblanched almonds
¼ cup golden seedless raisins (sultanas)
4 teaspoons moderately finely chopped crystallized ginger

This rich, moist cake always gets raves.

*P*reheat the oven to moderate (350° F.). Spray a 9-inch round cake pan with the cooking spray, line the bottom with wax paper, spray the paper, then add the 2 tablespoons flour and tilt the pan first to one side, then to another, until all surfaces are evenly coated with flour. Tap out any excess flour and set the pan aside.

For the Cake: Sift the flour, soda, cardamom, cinnamon, and salt onto a piece of wax paper and set aside. Beat the sugar and oil in the large bowl of an electric mixer at medium speed about 2 minutes to blend, then add the egg whites, one at a time, and beat well after each addition. Remove the bowl from the mixer and fold in the sifted dry ingredients, then the carrots, almonds, raisins, and ginger. Spoon the batter into the prepared pan.

*B*ake 30 minutes in the preheated oven, or until a toothpick inserted in the center comes out clean. Cool the cake upright in its pan on a wire rack for 20 minutes, then invert on a rack that has been sprayed with nonstick vegetable cooking spray; remove and discard the wax paper. When the cake has cooled to room temperature, turn right-side-up onto a second rack and set on a counter lined with wax paper (to catch the drips of glaze).

For the Glaze: Combine all ingredients in a small bowl, then spread smoothly over the top of the cake, letting it run down the sides. Let the glaze harden for about an hour before cutting the cake.

LEMON GLAZE:

---

1 cup sifted confectioners' sugar
*2 tablespoons freshly squeezed lemon
juice*
1 teaspoon finely grated lemon zest

PER SERVING: 251–209 C   3–2 g P   8.9–7.4
g TF (1.2–1 g SAT)   41–34 g CARB   166–139
mg S   0–0 mg CH

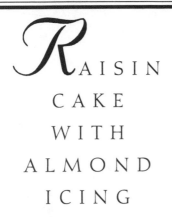

RAISIN CAKE WITH ALMOND ICING

MAKES A 9-INCH BUNDT CAKE,
24 SERVINGS

FOR PREPARING THE PAN:

Nonstick vegetable cooking spray
2 tablespoons all-purpose flour

CAKE:

2 cups sugar

2 cups hot water

¾ cup extra-light olive oil or vegetable
oil (canola, safflower, sunflower, corn oil,
etc.) blended with ¼ cup evaporated
skim milk

1½ cups seedless raisins

1½ cups golden seedless raisins
(sultanas)

2 teaspoons ground cinnamon

1 teaspoon ground cloves

½ teaspoon ground ginger

½ teaspoon freshly grated nutmeg

¼ teaspoon freshly ground black pepper

⅛ teaspoon salt

2 teaspoons baking soda

3½ cups sifted all-purpose flour

This unusual cake contains no eggs, but does contain pepper to "punch up" the flavor of the other spices. It's dense, dark, and delicious—a good, quick substitute for fruitcake.

Preheat the oven to moderate (350° F.). Liberally spray a 9-inch (12-cup) Bundt pan with the cooking spray, add the 2 tablespoons flour, and tilt the pan first to one side, then to the other, until all surfaces are evenly coated with flour. Tap out any excess flour and set the pan aside.

For the Cake: Place the sugar, water, oil-milk mixture, the raisins, cinnamon, cloves, ginger, nutmeg, pepper, and salt in a very large heavy saucepan. Set the pan over moderate heat, bring contents to a boil, then boil, uncovered, 1 minute. Remove from the heat and stir in the soda—the mixture will froth furiously. Cool to room temperature.

Stir in the flour, about ⅓ of the total amount at a time, then pour the batter into the prepared pan and bake 1 to 1¼ hours in the preheated oven until the cake begins to pull from the sides of the pan and the top springs back slowly when pressed with a finger. Cool the cake upright in its pan on a wire rack 10 minutes, then turn out on the rack and cool to room temperature.

For the Icing: Combine all ingredients, whisking until smooth. Line the counter with wax paper (to catch the drips), set the cake (still on the rack) on top, then drizzle the icing over the cake so that it runs down the sides like icicles. Let the icing harden 1 to 2 hours before cutting the cake.

> ### *ALMOND ICING:*
>
> ¾ *cup unsifted confectioners' sugar*
> 1 *tablespoon hot water*
> ½ *teaspoon almond extract*
> ½ *teaspoon vanilla*
>
> <u>PER SERVING</u>: 259 C   2 g P   7.3 g TF (1 g
> SAT)   48 g CARB   83 mg S   0 mg CH

MEXICAN CHOCOLATE CAKE

MAKES A 9-INCH ROUND CAKE,
10 SERVINGS

CAKE:

1⅞ cups sifted all-purpose flour

1 teaspoon baking soda

½ teaspoon baking powder

1 teaspoon ground cinnamon

¼ teaspoon ground ginger

⅛ teaspoon salt

⅔ cup firmly packed dark brown sugar

½ cup unsweetened Dutch process cocoa powder

½ cup hot water

½ cup lowfat buttermilk

½ cup cold water

⅓ cup extra-light olive oil or vegetable oil (canola, safflower, sunflower, corn oil, etc.)

2 teaspoons vanilla

3 egg whites

3 tablespoons granulated sugar

The cinnamon and ginger make all the difference.

Preheat the oven to moderate (350° F.). Liberally spray a 9-inch round cake pan with nonstick vegetable cooking spray and set aside.

For the Cake: Sift the flour, soda, baking powder, cinnamon, ginger, and salt into a large mixing bowl. Add the brown sugar and work it into the dry ingredients with your fingers, pressing out all lumps. Make a well in the center of the dry ingredients. In a 1-quart measuring cup, blend the cocoa and hot water, whisk in the buttermilk, cold water, oil, and vanilla and set aside. Quickly beat the egg whites until foamy, then add the granulated sugar gradually, beating all the while, until the mixture peaks softly.

Dump the oil mixture into the well in the dry ingredients and stir just enough to combine. Do not overmix or the cake will be tough. Now fold in about ¼ of the beaten whites to lighten the batter. Finally, fold in the balance of the egg whites. Pour the batter into the prepared pan.

Bake 35 minutes in the preheated oven, or until a toothpick inserted in the center of the cake comes out *just* clean—don't overbake. Cool the cake upright in its pan on a wire rack for 20 minutes, then invert on a rack that has been sprayed with nonstick vegetable cooking spray. When the cake has cooled to room temperature, turn right-side-up on a serving plate and set aside.

CHOCOLATE GLAZE:

1½ cups confectioners' sugar

3 tablespoons unsweetened Dutch
process cocoa powder

1½ tablespoons light corn syrup

2 tablespoons hot water

PER SERVING: 520 C   5 g P   8.9 g TF (1.8
g SAT)   59 g CARB   212 mg S
0.5 mg CH

For the Glaze: Combine all ingredients in the top of a double boiler set over simmering water and whisk just until the sugar dissolves and the mixture is creamy-smooth, about 5 minutes. Do not let the water boil at any time or the glaze will not be shiny. If the glaze seems too thick to pour, thin it with a little hot water. Pour the glaze over the cake, smoothing it to the edges and around the sides. Let the glaze harden before cutting the cake.

BLACK FOREST CAKE

MAKES AN 8-INCH ROUND CAKE,
8 SERVINGS

CAKE:

½ cup unsifted cake flour

¼ cup unsweetened Dutch process cocoa
powder

⅞ cup sugar

8 egg whites, at room temperature

½ teaspoon cream of tartar

1 teaspoon vanilla

FILLING:

2 tablespoons kirsch

1 teaspoon unflavored gelatin

1 (16-ounce) can water-packed, pitted
sour red cherries, drained (reserve liquid)

2 tablespoons granulated sugar

1 tablespoon cornstarch

½ cup cherry liquid (drained from the
can of cherries)

⅔ cup ice-cold evaporated skim milk

1 teaspoon freshly squeezed lemon juice

½ cup Labna (page 176), or lowfat
(1 percent) cottage cheese, puréed until
smooth

2 tablespoons confectioners' sugar

½ teaspoon vanilla

As made in Germany, this chocolate layer cake is sand-wiched together with gobs of whipped cream and frosted with even more of it. This low-fat, low-cholesterol version looks and tastes every bit as verboten.

Preheat the oven to moderately hot (375° F.). Line the bottoms of 2 (8-inch) round layer cake pans with wax paper. Do not grease the paper or the sides of the pans; set the pans aside.

For the Cake: Sift the flour and cocoa together 3 times, then sift once again with ½ cup of the sugar onto a piece of wax paper and set aside. Beat the egg whites with the cream of tartar to soft peaks. Add the remaining sugar, 1 tablespoon at a time, and continue beating until glossy and stiff. Fold in the vanilla. Sift ⅓ of the flour mixture over the beaten whites and fold in gently but thoroughly. Repeat twice more, until all of the flour mixture is incorporated. Divide the batter between the 2 prepared pans and smooth the surface. Bake the cakes in the preheated oven for 20 to 25 minutes, or until springy to the touch. Remove the cakes from the oven, invert at once on wire racks, and cool upside-down in the pans. When completely cool, loosen each cake around the edge with a thin-bladed spatula, turn out, and peel off the wax paper. Set the cakes aside while you prepare the filling.

For the Filling: Place the kirsch in a very small, heavy saucepan, sprinkle the gelatin on top and let stand 5 minutes. Set over very low heat and stir 2 to 3 minutes until the gelatin dissolves; work carefully because the kirsch may ignite. Remove from the heat and cool. Dump the cherries into a medium-size heatproof bowl and set aside also.

Combine the granulated sugar and cornstarch in a small saucepan, pressing out all lumps, then mix in the reserved cherry liquid. Set over moderate heat and cook, stirring constantly, 2 to 3 minutes, or until the mixture thickens and clears. Mix into the cherries and reserve.

*B*eat the evaporated milk and lemon juice in the smallest electric mixer bowl at high speed until very stiff. Meanwhile, in another small bowl, whisk the Labna with the confectioners' sugar and vanilla until smooth. Beat the cooled gelatin mixture into the whipped evaporated milk, then fold into the Labna mixture.

To Assemble the Cake: Place 1 cake layer on a small cake plate. Spread with the cherry mixture, pushing it right to the edge. Carefully spread 1 cup of the whipped evaporated milk mixture over the cherries, again right to the edge. Top with the second cake layer. Fit a pastry bag with a star tip and fill with the remaining whipped evaporated milk mixture. Pipe 8 rosettes around the top of the cake. Pipe any additional cream in a design in the center, if you like. Chill the cake until serving time; then, if you like, arrange the candied cherries in the rosettes on top of the cake and sprig each with the green candied cherry leaves. Cut into slim wedges and serve.

OPTIONAL GARNISHES:

8 candied red cherries
4 candied green cherries, cut into leaf shapes

<u>PER SERVING</u>: 241 C   8 g P   0.6 g TF (0.3 g SAT)   51 g CARB   115 mg S   0.8 mg CH

$\mathscr{B}$UTTERMILK P O U N D C A K E

MAKES A 9-INCH BUNDT CAKE,
12 SERVINGS

2⅓ cups sifted all-purpose flour
½ cup granulated sugar
1½ teaspoons baking powder
½ teaspoon baking soda
½ teaspoon freshly grated nutmeg
⅛ teaspoon salt
¾ cup firmly packed light brown sugar
½ cup extra-light olive oil or vegetable
oil (canola, safflower, sunflower, corn oil,
etc.)
¼ cup evaporated skim milk
1 cup lowfat buttermilk
2 teaspoons vanilla
1½ teaspoons butter flavor extract
3 egg whites

PER SERVING: 266 C   4 g P   9.9 g TF (1.5
g SAT)   41 g CARB   156 mg S   1 mg CH

If this cake is to have the proper flavor, you must use freshly grated nutmeg, not commercially ground, which sometimes has a bitter aftertaste.

Preheat the oven to moderate (350° F.). Liberally spray a 9-inch (8-cup) Bundt pan with nonstick vegetable cooking spray and set aside.

Sift the flour, ¼ cup of the granulated sugar, the baking powder, soda, nutmeg, and salt into a large mixing bowl. Add the brown sugar and mix well with your fingers, pressing out all lumps. Then make a well in the center of the dry ingredients. (Or, even easier, pulse the flour, granulated sugar, baking powder, soda, nutmeg, salt, and brown sugar 4 to 6 times in a food processor until uniformly fine. Transfer to a large mixing bowl and make a well in the center.)

In a 1-quart measuring cup, whisk the oil with the evaporated milk, buttermilk, vanilla, and butter extract until uniformly creamy. Beat the egg whites until foamy, gradually beat in the remaining ¼ cup granulated sugar, and continue beating to soft peaks. Quickly pour the oil mixture into the well in the dry ingredients and stir just to combine. The batter will be quite stiff, a bit lumpy, too, but do not beat any further at this point or the cake will be tough. Gently fold ¼ of the beaten whites into the batter to lighten it, then fold in the balance until no streaks of white or yellow remain. Spoon the batter into the prepared pan.

Bake the cake 50 minutes in the preheated oven or until a toothpick inserted near the center comes out clean. Cool the cake upright in its pan on a wire rack for 20 minutes, then loosen around the edge and central tube and invert on a wire rack that has been sprayed with nonstick vegetable cooking spray. Cool to room temperature before cutting.

CHOCOLATE POUND CAKE

MAKES A 9-INCH BUNDT CAKE,
16 SERVINGS

FOR PREPARING THE PAN:

Nonstick vegetable cooking spray
2 tablespoons unsweetened Dutch
process cocoa powder

CAKE:

2½ cups sifted all-purpose flour
2 cups unsifted confectioners' sugar
½ cup unsweetened Dutch process cocoa
powder
1¾ teaspoons baking powder
½ teaspoon baking soda
⅛ teaspoon salt
1⅓ cups granulated brown sugar
¾ cup extra-light olive oil or vegetable
oil (canola, safflower, sunflower, corn oil,
etc.)
1 cup liquid egg substitute
1¼ cups evaporated skim milk
½ cup water
1 tablespoon vanilla

OPTIONAL TOPPING:

1 tablespoon confectioners' sugar (for
dusting)

PER SERVING: 296 C 5 g P 11.5 g TF (1.9
g SAT) 46 g CARB 161 mg S
0.8 mg CH

---

*D*usting the pan with cocoa gives the cake a rich chocolaty finish.

*P*reheat the oven to moderate (350° F.). Spray a 9-inch (12-cup) Bundt pan with the cooking spray, add the 2 tablespoons cocoa, and tilt the pan first to one side, then to another, until all surfaces are evenly coated with cocoa. Tap out any excess cocoa and set the pan aside.

For the Cake: Sift the flour, confectioners' sugar, cocoa, baking powder, soda, and salt into a large mixing bowl. Add the brown sugar and mix well, then make a well in the center of the dry ingredients. (Or, even easier, pulse the flour, confectioners' sugar, cocoa, baking powder, soda, salt, and brown sugar 4 to 6 times in a food processor until uniformly fine. Transfer to a large mixing bowl and make a well in the center.)

In a 1-quart measuring cup, whisk the oil with the egg substitute, milk, water, and vanilla until uniformly creamy; pour into the well in the dry ingredients and stir briskly just enough to mix. The batter will be very thin and a bit lumpy, too, but do not beat any further at this point or the cake will be tough. Pour the batter into the prepared pan.

*B*ake 45 to 50 minutes in the preheated oven, or until a cake tester inserted near the center of the cake comes out clean. Cool the cake upright in its pan on a wire rack for 20 minutes, then loosen around the edge and central tube and invert on a wire rack that has been sprayed with nonstick vegetable cooking spray. Cool the cake to room temperature, then, if you like, dust with confectioners' sugar.

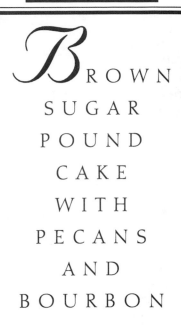

BROWN SUGAR POUND CAKE WITH PECANS AND BOURBON

MAKES A 10-INCH TUBE CAKE,
24 SERVINGS

FOR PREPARING THE PAN:

Nonstick vegetable cooking spray
2 tablespoons all-purpose flour

CAKE:

1 cup coarsely chopped pecans
3 cups sifted all-purpose flour
¾ cup granulated sugar
1 teaspoon baking powder
½ teaspoon baking soda
⅛ teaspoon salt
2½ cups granulated brown sugar
1 cup extra-light olive oil or vegetable oil
(canola, safflower, sunflower, corn oil,
etc.)

Walnuts, black walnuts, even skinned, toasted hazelnuts can be substituted for the pecans in this moist, compact cake. Just make sure the nuts you use are good and fresh. Unfortunately, the nuts sold these days in little cellophane packets are sometimes rancid, so taste them before using, and reject any that are stale.

Preheat the oven to moderately slow (325° F.). Spray a 10-inch tube pan with the cooking spray, add the 2 tablespoons flour, and tilt the pan first to one side then to another, until all surfaces are evenly coated with flour. Tap out any excess flour and set the pan aside.

For the Cake: Toss the pecans with ¼ cup of the flour and set aside. Sift the remaining flour, ½ cup of the granulated sugar, the baking powder, soda, and salt into a large mixing bowl. Add the brown sugar, toss well to mix, then make a well in the center of the dry ingredients. (Or, even easier, pulse the flour, granulated sugar, baking powder, soda, salt, and brown sugar 4 to 6 times in a food processor until uniformly fine. Transfer to a large mixing bowl and make a well in the center.)

In a 1-quart measuring cup, whisk the oil with the milk, egg substitute, bourbon, and vanilla until uniformly creamy. Beat the egg whites until foamy, gradually beat in the remaining ¼ cup granulated sugar, and continue beating to soft peaks. Quickly pour the oil mixture into the well in the dry ingredients and stir just to combine. The batter will be a bit lumpy, but do not beat any further at this point or the cake will be tough. Gently fold ¼ of the beaten whites into the batter to lighten it, then fold in the balance until no streaks of white or brown remain. Finally, fold in the pecans and their dredging flour—easy does it. Pour the batter into the prepared pan.

1 cup evaporated skim milk
⅓ cup liquid egg substitute
¼ cup bourbon
1 teaspoon vanilla
4 egg whites

PER SERVING: 266 C   4 g P   12.9 g TF (1.6
g SAT)   36 g CARB   77 mg S   0.4 mg CH

$\mathscr{B}$ake the cake 1 hour and 15 to 20 minutes in the preheated oven or until a toothpick inserted near the center comes out clean. Cool the cake upright in its pan on a wire rack for 10 minutes, then loosen around the edge and central tube and invert on the rack. Cool to room temperature before cutting into slim wedges.

APPLE-YOGURT COFFEE CAKE WITH STREUSEL TOPPING

MAKES A 9-INCH ROUND CAKE,
12 SERVINGS

FOR PREPARING THE PAN:

Nonstick vegetable cooking spray
2 tablespoons all-purpose flour

CAKE:

1⅔ cups sifted all-purpose flour
1 cup sugar
¾ teaspoon baking powder
½ teaspoon baking soda
Pinch of salt
⅓ cup extra-light olive oil or vegetable oil (canola, safflower, sunflower, corn oil, etc.)
⅓ cup evaporated skim milk
¾ cup plain nonfat yogurt
1 teaspoon vanilla
4 egg whites
1 medium-size tart apple, peeled, cored, and sliced very thin

*P*reheat the oven to moderate (350° F.). Spray a 9-inch springform pan with the cooking spray, line the bottom with wax paper, spray the paper, then add the 2 tablespoons flour and tilt the pan first to one side, then to another, until all the surfaces are evenly coated with flour. Tap out any excess flour and set the pan aside.

For the Cake: Sift the flour, ¾ cup of the sugar, the baking powder, soda, and salt into a large mixing bowl and make a well in the center. Whisk the oil with the milk, yogurt, and vanilla in a 1-quart measuring cup until creamy and set aside. Quickly beat the egg whites until foamy, then add the remaining ¼ cup sugar gradually, beating all the while, until the mixture peaks softly.

*D*ump the oil mixture into the well in the dry ingredients and stir just enough to make a very stiff batter. Do not overmix or the cake will be tough. Fold in about ¼ of the beaten whites to lighten the batter, then fold in the balance, gently but thoroughly, until no streaks of white or yellow show. Spoon ½ the batter into the prepared pan, arrange the apple slices on top, then cover with the remaining batter.

For the Streusel: Combine all ingredients by pulsing quickly in a food processor and scatter on top of the batter.

*B*ake in the preheated oven 40 to 45 minutes, or until a toothpick inserted in the center of the cake comes out clean. *Note: If after 20 minutes the streusel topping is browning too fast, cover the cake with foil.* When the cake tests done, cool upright in its pan on a wire rack for 10 minutes, then release the springform sides and remove. Cool the cake completely on the rack before serving.

STREUSEL TOPPING:

3 tablespoons unsifted all-purpose flour
2 tablespoons granulated brown sugar
1 teaspoon butter flavor granules
½ teaspoon ground cinnamon
1 tablespoon extra-light olive oil
¼ cup moderately coarsely chopped walnuts

PER SERVING: 247 C   5 g P   9.2 g TF (1.2 g SAT)   37 g CARB   124 mg S   0.6 mg CH

OAT CRUNCH COFFEE CAKE

MAKES A 13 × 9 × 2-INCH LOAF
CAKE, 12 SERVINGS

CAKE:

1¾ cups sifted all-purpose flour

1 cup sugar

2 teaspoons baking powder

½ teaspoon baking soda

¾ teaspoon ground cinnamon

¼ teaspoon ground allspice

⅛ teaspoon ground cloves

Pinch of freshly grated nutmeg

¼ cup plus 1 tablespoon extra-light olive
oil or vegetable oil (canola, safflower,
sunflower, corn oil, etc.)

1 cup plain nonfat yogurt

1 teaspoon vanilla

3 egg whites

TOPPING:

¼ cup old-fashioned rolled oats

¼ cup unsifted all-purpose flour

¼ cup firmly packed dark brown sugar

1½ teaspoons butter flavor granules

1½ tablespoons extra-light olive oil or
vegetable oil (canola, safflower,
sunflower, corn oil, etc.)

PER SERVING: 242 C   4 g P   7.9 g TF (1.1 g
SAT)   39 g CARB   157 mg S   0.5 mg CH

Not too sweet, this cake is good for breakfast or with an afternoon cup of tea.

Preheat the oven to moderate (350° F.). Lightly spray a 13 × 9 × 2-inch loaf pan with nonstick vegetable cooking spray and set aside.

For the Cake: Sift the flour, ¾ cup of the sugar, the baking powder, soda, cinnamon, allspice, cloves, and nutmeg into a large mixing bowl and make a well in the center. In a 1-quart measuring cup, whisk the oil with the yogurt and vanilla until uniformly creamy. Beat the egg whites until foamy, gradually beat in the remaining ¼ cup sugar, and continue beating to soft peaks. Quickly pour the oil mixture into the well in the dry ingredients and stir just to combine. The batter will be quite stiff and lumpy but do not mix any further at this point or the cake will be tough. Gently fold ¼ of the beaten whites into the batter to lighten it, then fold in the balance until no streaks of white or tan remain. Spoon the batter into the prepared pan, then smooth into a thin layer, spreading well into the corners.

For the Topping: Pulse the rolled oats, flour, brown sugar, butter granules, and oil in a food processor just until crumbly, then sprinkle evenly over the batter.

Bake the coffee cake 40 to 45 minutes in the preheated oven, or until a toothpick inserted in the center of the cake comes out clean. Cool the coffee cake upright in its pan on a wire rack to room temperature. Cut into large squares and serve.

CLOCKWISE FROM TOP RIGHT:
*M*ARBLEIZED *C*HOCOLATE-
*A*LMOND *C*HEESE *P*IE *(page 70)*,
*L*OW-CHOLESTEROL *C*HEESE
*P*IE *(page 68)*,
*G*LAZED *O*RANGE *T*OFU
*C*HEESECAKE *(page 72)*

FROZEN FUDGE MOUSSE
WITH HOT FUDGE SAUCE
AND MOCK WHIPPED CREAM
(page 158)

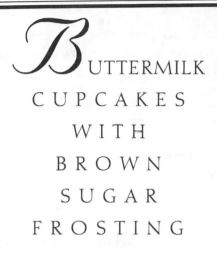

$\mathcal{B}$UTTERMILK CUPCAKES WITH BROWN SUGAR FROSTING

MAKES 12

CUPCAKES:

1 cup sifted all-purpose flour
⅔ cup sugar
¾ teaspoon baking powder
¼ teaspoon baking soda
Pinch of salt
¼ cup extra-light olive oil or vegetable oil (canola, safflower, sunflower, corn oil, etc.)
½ cup liquid egg substitute
⅔ cup lowfat buttermilk
1 teaspoon vanilla
1 teaspoon butter flavor extract

BROWN SUGAR FROSTING:

2 tablespoons unsalted soft tub margarine (not extra-light)
¼ cup firmly packed dark brown sugar
½ cup unsifted confectioners' sugar
1½ teaspoons freshly squeezed lemon juice

PER CUPCAKE: 183 C   2 g P   6.7 g TF (1 g SAT)   29 g CARB   84 mg S   0.5 mg CH

$\mathcal{P}$reheat the oven to moderate (350° F.). Line 12 muffin pan cups with crinkly paper liners and set aside.

For the Cupcakes: Sift the flour, sugar, baking powder, soda, and salt into a large mixing bowl and make a well in the center. Whisk the oil with the egg substitute, the buttermilk, vanilla, and butter extract in a 1-quart measuring cup until creamy, pour into the well in the dry ingredients, and stir just enough to mix. The batter will be very thin, a bit lumpy, too, but do not stir any further at this point or the cupcakes will be tough.

$\mathcal{S}$poon the batter into the prepared muffin pans, making each cup no more than ⅔ full. Bake 20 minutes in the preheated oven, or until a toothpick inserted in the center of a cupcake comes out clean. Cool the cupcakes upright in their pans for 10 minutes on a wire rack, then remove from the pans and cool on the rack to room temperature.

For the Frosting: In the small bowl of an electric mixer set at high speed, beat the margarine, brown sugar, confectioners' sugar, and lemon juice until both creamy and fluffy—about 2 to 3 minutes. Frost the top of each cupcake, then let the frosting harden about an hour before serving.

ZERO-CHOLESTEROL BROWNIES

MAKES 12 (2⅔ × 2-INCH) BROWNIES

1 cup sifted all-purpose flour
6 tablespoons unsweetened Dutch process cocoa powder
1 cup sugar
½ cup moderately coarsely chopped pecans or walnuts
¼ cup extra-light olive oil or vegetable oil (canola, safflower, sunflower, corn oil, etc.) blended with ¼ cup evaporated skim milk
⅔ cup liquid egg substitute
¼ cup light corn syrup
1½ teaspoons vanilla
1 teaspoon butter flavor extract

PER BROWNIE: 204 C   3 g P   8.4 g TF (1.2 g SAT)   31 g CARB   47 mg S   0 mg CH

Dark and oh, so moist and chewy!

Preheat the oven to moderate (350° F.). Spray an 8 × 8 × 2-inch pan with nonstick vegetable cooking spray and set aside.

Sift the flour, cocoa, and sugar into a large mixing bowl, add the pecans, and toss well to dredge. Make a well in the center. In a 1-quart measuring cup, whisk the oil mixture with the egg substitute, corn syrup, vanilla, and butter extract, pour into the well in the dry ingredients, and stir just enough to mix. Pour the batter into the prepared pan.

Bake 30 minutes in the preheated oven, or until springy to the touch. Cool the brownies upright in their pan on a wire rack for 20 minutes, then invert on the rack, turn right-side-up, and cool to room temperature. Cut into 12 bars (approximately 2⅔ × 2 inches).

RAISIN- PECAN BARS

MAKES 16 (2¼ × 2¼-INCH) BARS

2¼ cups sifted all-purpose flour
1 cup firmly packed dark brown sugar
½ cup granulated sugar
1½ teaspoons baking powder
½ cup golden seedless raisins (sultanas)
½ cup coarsely chopped pecans or
walnuts
¾ cup liquid egg substitute
⅓ cup extra-light olive oil or vegetable
oil (canola, safflower, sunflower, corn oil,
etc.)
¼ cup evaporated skim milk
1½ teaspoons vanilla

PER BAR: 220 C   3 g P   7.1 g TF (0.8 g
SAT)   37 g CARB   65 mg S   0.2 mg CH

*P*reheat the oven to moderate (350° F.). Spray a 9 × 9 × 2-inch pan with nonstick vegetable cooking spray and set aside.

*P*ulse the flour, brown sugar, granulated sugar, and baking powder in a food processor 4 to 6 times until uniformly fine. Add the raisins and pecans and pulse 2 to 3 times to dredge; then empty into a large mixing bowl and make a well in the center. Whisk the egg substitute with the oil, milk, and vanilla in a 1-quart measuring cup until creamy. Pour the liquid into the well in the dry ingredients and stir just to mix—no more or the bars will be tough. Spoon the batter into the prepared pan, smoothing it to the corners.

*B*ake 40 to 45 minutes in the preheated oven, or until a toothpick inserted in the center comes out *just* clean. Cool upright in the pan on a wire rack for 30 minutes, then cut into 16 (2¼-inch) squares.

CINNAMON-PUMPKIN BARS

MAKES 18 (3 × 2¼-INCH) BARS

2 cups sifted all-purpose flour
2 teaspoons baking powder
1 teaspoon baking soda
1½ teaspoons ground cinnamon
½ teaspoon ground ginger
½ teaspoon ground cloves
½ teaspoon freshly grated nutmeg
1½ cups sugar
¾ cup liquid egg substitute
⅔ cup extra-light olive oil or vegetable
oil (canola, safflower, sunflower, corn oil,
etc.)
¼ cup evaporated skim milk
1 (16-ounce) can solid pack pumpkin
(not pie mix)

TOPPING:

1 tablespoon sugar mixed with ½
teaspoon ground cinnamon

PER BAR: 203 C   3 g P   8.7 g TF (1.3 g
SAT)   30 g CARB   112 mg S   0.1 mg CH

These low-saturated-fat, low-cholesterol bars are rich in beta-carotene, which the body converts into vitamin A.

Preheat the oven to moderately slow (325° F.). Spray a 13 × 9 × 2-inch pan with nonstick vegetable cooking spray and set aside.

Sift the flour, baking powder, soda, cinnamon, ginger, cloves, nutmeg, and sugar into a large mixing bowl and make a well in the center. In a 1-quart measure, whisk the egg substitute with the oil, milk, and pumpkin until well blended. Pour into the well in the dry ingredients, and stir just enough to combine. The batter will be lumpy, but do not mix further at this point or the bars will be tough. Spoon the batter into the prepared pan, spreading it well into the corners and smoothing the top, then sprinkle the topping evenly over all.

Bake 40 to 45 minutes in the preheated oven, or until a toothpick inserted in the center comes out just clean. Cool upright in the pan on a wire rack for 30 minutes, then cut into 18 bars approximately 3 inches long and 2¼ inches wide.

SPICY OATMEAL-RAISIN COOKIES

MAKES ABOUT 3½ DOZEN

1½ cups unsifted all-purpose flour
1½ teaspoons baking powder
¾ teaspoon ground cinnamon
½ teaspoon ground ginger
¼ teaspoon freshly grated nutmeg
¼ teaspoon ground cloves
¾ cup firmly packed light brown sugar
½ cup extra-light olive oil or vegetable oil (canola, safflower, sunflower, corn oil, etc.)
⅓ cup liquid egg substitute
3 tablespoons skim milk
1 cup quick-cooking rolled oats
¾ cup seedless raisins
½ cup coarsely chopped pecans or walnuts

PER COOKIE: 79 C   1 g P   3.7 g TF (0.5 g SAT)   11 g CARB   17 mg S   0 mg CH

This is one of the few cookie recipes that uses vegetable oil in place of butter, shortening, or even margarine. It contains no cholesterol, almost no saturated fat, and compared with most cookies, very little fat, period.

Preheat the oven to moderate (350° F.). Sift the flour, baking powder, and spices into a large bowl, add the brown sugar, and work it in with your hands until uniformly fine and crumbly. Make a well in the middle of the dry ingredients. In a large measuring cup, whisk the oil with the egg substitute and milk until smooth. Pour into the well in the dry ingredients and mix just enough to combine. Stir in the oats, raisins, and pecans.

Drop by rounded teaspoonfuls onto baking sheets lightly sprayed with nonstick vegetable cooking spray, spacing 2 inches apart and bake on the middle shelf of the preheated oven for 10 to 12 minutes until lightly browned. Cool 1 minute on the baking sheets, then remove to wire racks. When completely cool, store airtight.

$\mathcal{L}$ACY OATMEAL COOKIES

MAKES ABOUT 5 DOZEN

½ cup sifted all-purpose flour
¼ teaspoon baking powder
½ cup sugar
½ cup old-fashioned rolled oats
2 tablespoons evaporated skim milk
2 tablespoons light corn syrup
4 tablespoons plus 1½ teaspoons extra-light olive oil or vegetable oil (canola, safflower, sunflower, corn oil, etc.)
2 teaspoons vanilla
1 teaspoon orange extract

PER COOKIE: 25 C   LESS THAN 1 g P
1.1 g TF (0.2 g SAT)   3 g CARB   3 mg S
0 mg CH

$\mathcal{T}$hese shattery-crisp cookies taste for all the world as if they're loaded with chopped almonds. But they contain no high-fat nuts at all.

$\mathcal{P}$reheat the oven to moderately hot (375° F.). Mix the flour, baking powder, sugar, and oats in a small mixing bowl and make a well in the center. Whisk the milk, corn syrup, oil, vanilla, and orange extract in a 2-cup measure until creamy, dump into the well in the dry ingredients, and stir just enough to mix. Drop by rounded ¼ teaspoonfuls onto baking sheets sprayed with nonstick vegetable cooking spray, spacing the cookies at least 3 inches apart. The cookies will spread considerably during baking. Bake in the preheated oven for 6 to 8 minutes until a nice caramel brown. Cool on the baking sheets about 1 minute until the cookies firm up a bit, then using a spatula sprayed with nonstick vegetable cooking spray, transfer them to wire racks to cool completely. Store airtight.

$\mathcal{P}$RALINE CRISPS

MAKES ABOUT 5 DOZEN

2¼ cups sifted all-purpose flour
2 cups firmly packed light brown sugar
½ teaspoon baking soda
1 cup coarsely chopped pecans
⅓ cup extra-light olive oil or vegetable oil (canola, safflower, sunflower, corn oil, etc.)
⅓ cup liquid egg substitute
3 tablespoons evaporated skim milk
1½ teaspoons vanilla
1 teaspoon butter flavor extract

PER COOKIE: 63 C   1 g P   2.5 g TF (0.3 g SAT)   9 g CARB   11 mg S   0 mg CH

$\mathcal{O}$f all the cookies my mother made, these were my favorites. Her recipe, alas, didn't skimp on butter or eggs. But I've managed to work out a more healthful version, which, I promise, is every bit as crisp and delicious as the original.

$\mathcal{P}$reheat the oven to moderate (350° F.). Pulse the flour, sugar, and soda 8 to 10 times in a food processor until uniformly fine; add the nuts and pulse 3 to 4 times to dredge. Empty into a large mixing bowl and make a well in the center. Whisk the oil with the egg substitute, milk, vanilla, and butter extract in a 1-quart measuring cup until creamy; pour into the well in the dry ingredients and stir only enough to mix (the dough will be very stiff). Drop by rounded teaspoonfuls onto baking sheets lightly sprayed with nonstick vegetable cooking spray, spacing about 2 inches apart. Bake 10 to 12 minutes in the preheated oven until lightly browned. Transfer at once to wire racks to cool. Store airtight.

SOFT GINGER COOKIES

MAKES ABOUT 4 DOZEN

2½ cups unsifted all-purpose flour
1 teaspoon baking powder
½ teaspoon baking soda
1 teaspoon ground ginger
½ teaspoon ground cinnamon
¼ teaspoon ground cloves
¼ teaspoon freshly grated nutmeg
½ cup firmly packed dark brown sugar
⅓ cup extra-light olive oil or vegetable oil (canola, safflower, sunflower, corn oil, etc.)
½ cup boiling water
½ cup molasses
¼ cup liquid egg substitute

PER COOKIE: 55 C   1 G P   1.6 G TF (0.2 G SAT)   9 G CARB   20 MG S   0 MG CH

The batter for these cookies is almost as thin as cake batter, but the cookies are wonderfully plump and chewy—little pillows of spice.

Preheat the oven to moderate (350° F.). Sift the flour, baking powder, soda, and spices together into a large bowl. Add the sugar, mix well with your hands until uniformly crumbly, then make a well in the center of the dry ingredients. In a 1-quart measuring cup, combine the oil, water, and molasses, whisking until smooth, then pour into the well in the dry ingredients and beat just enough to mix. Stir in the egg substitute.

Drop by level tablespoonfuls onto baking sheets lightly sprayed with nonstick vegetable cooking spray, spacing 2 inches apart. Smooth each cookie into a round. Bake 10 to 12 minutes in the preheated oven until edged with brown. Transfer at once to wire racks to cool. Store airtight.

ORANGE-ALMOND ICEBOX COOKIES

MAKES ABOUT 5 DOZEN

2¾ cups sifted all-purpose flour
¼ teaspoon baking soda
¼ cup granulated sugar
½ cup firmly packed light brown sugar
1 cup coarsely chopped blanched almonds
⅓ cup extra-light olive oil or vegetable oil (canola, safflower, sunflower, corn oil, etc.)
¼ cup liquid egg substitute
5 tablespoons freshly squeezed orange juice
1 tablespoon finely grated orange zest
1 teaspoon vanilla
½ teaspoon almond extract

PER COOKIE: 54 C 1 g P 2.4 g TF (0.3 g SAT) 7 g CARB 6 mg S 0 mg CH

This tender dough must be very cold if it is to slice neatly. Whenever I'm in a hurry, I give the rolls of dough 2½ to 3 hours in the freezer instead of overnight in the refrigerator.

Sift the flour, soda, and granulated sugar into a large bowl, add the brown sugar, and, using your hands, press out all lumps. Add the almonds and toss well to dredge, then make a well in the center of the dry ingredients. In a 1-quart measuring cup, whisk the oil with the egg substitute, orange juice and zest, the vanilla, and the almond extract until creamy; pour into the well in the dry ingredients and mix well.

Divide the dough in half and, with lightly floured hands, shape each half on a piece of wax paper into a log about 10 inches long and 1½ inches in diameter. Roll up, then overwrap in heavy-duty aluminum foil, and chill until firm enough to slice thin—2½ to 3 hours in the freezer or overnight in the refrigerator.

Preheat the oven to moderately hot (375° F.). Slice the logs of dough ¼ inch thick and space the cookies 2 inches apart on baking sheets lightly sprayed with nonstick vegetable cooking spray. Bake 10 to 12 minutes in the preheated oven until lightly ringed with brown. Cool on the baking sheets about 30 seconds, then transfer to wire racks. When completely cool, store airtight.

VARIATION:

Lemon-Walnut Icebox Cookies: Prepare as directed but substitute 2 teaspoons finely grated lemon zest for the orange zest and 1 cup coarsely chopped lightly toasted walnuts or pecans for the almonds. Do not substitute lemon juice for the orange juice.

PER COOKIE: 54 C 1 g P 2.5 g TF (0.3 g SAT) 7 g CARB 6 mg S 0 mg CH

LEBKUCHEN

MAKES ABOUT 4 DOZEN

LEBKUCHEN:

3½ cups sifted all-purpose flour (about)

½ teaspoon baking soda

1 teaspoon ground cinnamon

¾ teaspoon freshly grated nutmeg

½ teaspoon ground cloves

½ teaspoon ground allspice

¾ cup firmly packed dark brown sugar

½ cup moderately coarsely chopped blanched almonds

½ cup finely diced mixed candied fruits

¼ cup liquid egg substitute

½ cup honey

½ cup molassses

SNOWY GLAZE:

3 cups unsifted confectioners' sugar

2 tablespoons freshly squeezed lemon juice

2 tablespoons skim milk or evaporated skim milk

½ teaspoon finely grated lemon zest

1 teaspoon vanilla

PER COOKIE: 104 C   1 g P   1 g TF   (0.1 g SAT)   24 g CARB   23 mg S   0 mg CH

These German Christmas cookies contain no shortening at all, which makes them the perfect choice for those watching their fat and cholesterol consumption. They are chewy-firm, not crisp. Note: This cookie dough must chill for 24 hours before it's rolled.

For the Lebkuchen: Sift the flour, soda, cinnamon, nutmeg, cloves and allspice into a large bowl; add the sugar, and, using your fingers, press out all the lumps. Add the almonds and candied fruits and toss well to dredge. Make a well in the center of the dry ingredients. In a 1-quart measuring cup, whisk the egg substitute with the honey and molasses until creamy. Pour into the well in the dry ingredients and stir just enough to mix (if the dough seems soft or sticky, work in a little extra flour). Shape the dough into a round, flat loaf, wrap in heavy-duty aluminum foil and chill for 24 hours so that the flavors have a chance to mellow.

When ready to roll the dough, preheat the oven to moderate (350° F.). Roll the dough about as thin as piecrust (⅜ inch thick), about ¼ of the total amount at a time, on a lightly floured pastry cloth with a lightly floured, stockinette-covered rolling pin. Using lightly floured star- or heart- or other-shaped cookie cutters measuring about 3 inches across at the widest point, cut the dough into fancy shapes, then space about 1 inch apart on cookie sheets lightly sprayed with nonstick vegetable cooking spray.

Bake the cookies in the preheated over 8 to 10 minutes, just until they are soft-firm and very pale tan. Don't overbake, or the cookies will be tough. Cool on the baking sheet about 1 minute, then transfer to wire racks to cool completely.

For the Glaze: Whisk all ingredients together; then, using a large pastry brush, paint the top of each cookie with a thick layer of glaze. Let the glaze harden for about 1 hour before serving the cookies. *Note: Stored airtight, these cookies will remain remarkably fresh-tasting for about a month.*

Date Pinwheels

MAKES ABOUT 4½ DOZEN

DOUGH:

2 cups sifted all-purpose flour

1 cup firmly packed light brown sugar

¼ teaspoon baking soda

½ teaspoon ground cinnamon

¼ teaspoon freshly grated nutmeg

⅛ teaspoon ground allspice

¼ cup extra-light olive oil or vegetable oil (canola, safflower, sunflower, corn oil, etc.)

¼ cup liquid egg substitute

3 tablespoons evaporated skim milk

DATE FILLING:

2⅓ cups moderately finely diced pitted dates (about 10 ounces)

½ cup cold water

2 tablespoons sugar

1 tablespoon freshly squeezed lemon juice

PER COOKIE: 57 C   1 g P   1.1 g TF   (0.1 g SAT)   12 g CARB   8 mg S   0 mg CH

*Y*ou can make this cookie dough zip-quick in a food processor, but you must then season it overnight in the refrigerator so that its flavors will mellow. The dough will also firm up, making it easier to roll. The raw cookie rolls freeze beautifully and are good to have on hand—all you have to do is slice and bake as directed.

For the Dough: Pulse the flour, sugar, soda, cinnamon, nutmeg, and allspice in a food processor 8 to 10 times until uniformly fine. Whisk the oil with the egg substitute and milk in a large measuring cup until creamy, drizzle over the surface of the dry ingredients in the food processor, and pulse 6 to 8 times to make a stiff dough. It will seem quite crumbly, but will stick together when you pinch a bit of it together. *Note: If you don't have a food processor, simply combine all dry ingredients in a large bowl, then combine all liquid ingredients in a large measuring cup. Drizzle the combined liquids over the dry ingredients, tossing with a fork until uniformly crumbly.* Divide the dough in half, flatten each half into a 4-inch square, wrap snugly in heavy-duty aluminum foil, and chill in the refrigerator overnight, or better yet, for 24 hours.

When You Are Ready to Proceed, Prepare the Date Filling: Place all ingredients in a small heavy saucepan, cover, and simmer over very low heat, stirring now and then, for 10 minutes. Remove from the heat and beat with a wooden spoon until very thick and pasty. Cool to room temperature.

*U*sing a lightly floured stockinette-covered rolling pin, roll ½ the dough on lightly floured wax paper laid on top of a pastry cloth (this helps anchor the paper) into a 10-inch square about ⅛ inch thick. Trim and patch the dough as needed to make a perfect 10-inch square. Spread ½ the filling smoothly over the square, not quite to the edges. Beginning with the side facing you and lifting the wax paper to encourage the dough to roll up on itself, roll the dough and filling up together, jelly-roll style, as tight as possible. Wrap the wax paper around the dough, lay it across a large square of heavy-duty aluminum foil, and roll up in the foil, twirling the foil ends as you go to compact the roll of dough. Set in the freezer. Repeat with the remaining filling and dough.

*A*fter 5 hours in the freezer, the dough will be firm enough to cut neatly. Preheat the oven to moderate (350° F.). Slice the rolls of dough ¼ inch thick and space the cookies 2 inches apart on baking sheets lightly sprayed with nonstick vegetable cooking spray. Bake in the preheated oven for 10 to 12 minutes until the cookies begin to firm up. Remove from the oven and cool 5 minutes on the baking sheets. Carefully transfer the cookies to wire racks to cool, then store airtight.

V A R I A T I O N S :

Apricot Pinwheels (about 4½ dozen): Prepare as directed, substituting dried apricots for the dates and increasing the amount of sugar in the filling to ¼ cup. Also add ¼ teaspoon almond extract to the filling.

PER COOKIE: 57 C 1 g P 1.1 g TF (0.1 g SAT) 11 g CARB 8 mg S 0 mg CH

Prune Pinwheels (about 4½ dozen): Prepare as directed, substituting pitted prunes for the dates and increasing the amount of sugar in the filling to ¼ cup. Also decrease the amount of water in the filling to ⅓ cup.

PER COOKIE: 57 C 1 g P 1.1 g TF (0.1 g SAT) 12 g CARB 8 mg S 0 mg CH

$\mathcal{V}$ANILLE-KIPFERL (GERMAN VANILLA CRESCENTS)

MAKES ABOUT 4 DOZEN

½ cup superfine sugar

1½ cups slivered blanched almonds

1½ cups skinned, toasted hazelnuts (for
directions on toasting and skinning
hazelnuts, see the headnote for
Chocolate-Hazelnut Dacquoise, page 92)

¼ cup hazelnut or walnut oil

3 teaspoons vanilla

⅓ cup liquid egg substitute

6 tablespoons evaporated skim milk

1⅔ cups sifted cornstarch

1 cup sifted all-purpose flour

1 cup vanilla sugar for dredging the
cookies (see headnote)

PER COOKIE: 106 C 2 g P 5.8 g
TF (0.5 g SAT) 12 g CARB 6 mg S
0.1 mg CH

It wasn't easy to trim these melt-in-your-mouth cookies of all butter or margarine (my mother's recipe contained 1½ sticks) and have them still tender. I've managed it by substituting cornstarch for about ⅔ of the flour, also by grinding the nuts to paste to capitalize on the shortening power of their natural oils. Note: To make vanilla sugar, fill a 1-pint preserving jar with confectioners' sugar, then tuck in 2 vanilla beans that have been split lengthwise. Screw the lid down tight and let the sugar season about a week before using it. Stored tightly capped, vanilla sugar will keep almost indefinitely. It's delicious dusted over fresh fruits, cakes, and cookies. You can also use it in place of plain confectioners' sugar in most recipes. *This cookie dough must season overnight in the refrigerator before it's shaped, so plan accordingly.*

Churn the superfine sugar, almonds, hazelnuts, and hazelnut oil in a food processor 4 to 5 minutes, scraping the work bowl sides down 2 to 3 times, until the nuts are reduced to a smooth paste—it will be considerably thicker than peanut butter. Add the vanilla, egg substitute, and milk and pulse 6 to 8 times to incorporate. Dump in the cornstarch and flour and pulse 10 to 12 times to make a very stiff dough (it will be crumbly but should hold together when you pinch a bit of it together; if not, pulse in a few extra drops of evaporated skim milk). Scoop the dough onto a large square of heavy-duty aluminum foil, pat into a large flat loaf, wrap snugly, then refrigerate to let the dough "season" overnight.

When ready to shape the cookies, preheat the oven to moderately hot (375° F.). Using your hands, pinch off 1-inch chunks of dough and shape them into little crescents about 2¾ inches long and ¾ inch wide at the widest point. The dough is unusually crumbly, so you will have to pinch and squeeze it as you shape it. Space the cookies 1 inch apart on baking sheets lightly sprayed with non-stick vegetable cooking spray.

*B*ake 10 to 12 minutes in the preheated oven until pale tan and soft-firm (don't overbake or the cookies will be tough). Remove at once to wire racks. Place the vanilla sugar in a medium-size bowl and roll the still-warm cookies in it to coat evenly. Transfer to wire racks set over wax paper and sift any remaining vanilla sugar on top. Cool the cookies to room temperature, then layer into metal cookie tins, separating the layers with wax paper. Store airtight.

ALMOND SUSPIROS

MAKES ABOUT 3½ DOZEN

FOR PREPARING THE BAKING SHEETS:

Nonstick vegetable cooking spray
2 rounded tablespoons all-purpose flour

FOR THE SUSPIROS:

¾ cup slivered blanched almonds
⅔ cup sifted granulated sugar
1 cup sifted confectioners' sugar
¾ cup egg whites (about 5 extra-large eggs)
1½ teaspoons vanilla

PER COOKIE: 41 C 1 g P 1.4 g TF (0.1 g SAT) 7 g CARB 8 mg S 0 mg CH

In Portuguese, suspiro *means "sigh," and it's an apt name for these airy little egg-white puffs that are so popular throughout Portugal. They contain zero cholesterol and no fat other than that which occurs naturally in the almonds. For best results, choose a dry, sunny day for making suspiros.*

Preheat the oven to moderately slow (325° F.). Spray 2 large baking sheets liberally with nonstick vegetable cooking spray, then place 1 tablespoon of the flour on each sheet and tilt from side to side until evenly dusted; tap off all excess flour and set the baking sheets aside.

For the Suspiros: Spread the almonds in an ungreased 9-inch pie tin and toast 8 to 10 minutes in the preheated oven until golden brown. Remove from the oven and immediately reduce the temperature to very slow (275° F.). Cool the almonds to room temperature, then chop very coarsely and reserve. Measure out 3 tablespoons of the granulated sugar and set aside; sift the remaining granulated sugar twice with the confectioners' sugar and set aside also. Beat the egg whites with the vanilla at high mixer speed until frothy, add the 3 tablespoons reserved granulated sugar, 1 tablespoon at a time, then continue beating to almost-stiff peaks. With the mixer at moderate speed, beat in 4 tablespoons of the confectioners' sugar mixture, 1 tablespoon at a time. Sift the remaining sugar mixture on top of the beaten whites and fold it in gently but thoroughly. Finally, fold in the reserved almonds. Drop by rounded tablespoonfuls onto the prepared baking sheets, spacing the cookies about 1½ inches apart. Bake in the preheated oven for 1 hour, placing 1 baking sheet slightly above the middle of the oven and the second one 4 to 5 inches below; reverse the position of the baking sheets at halftime. If the *suspiros* begin to brown (they should never be darker than pale ivory, even when done), reduce the oven temperature to 250° F. After the *suspiros* have baked for 1 hour, turn the oven off and let them remain in the oven for 2 hours more. Gently twist the *suspiros* off the baking sheets or remove with a pancake turner, then, to keep them nice and crisp, store airtight.

Hazelnut
MERINGUES

MAKES ABOUT 4 ½ DOZEN

¾ cup sugar

¼ cup liquid egg substitute

½ teaspoon vanilla

1 cup very finely chopped, skinned,
toasted hazelnuts (for directions on
toasting hazelnuts, see the headnote for
Chocolate-Hazelnut Dacquoise, page 92)

2 tablespoons cornstarch

2 extra-large egg whites

PER COOKIE: 27 C   1 g P   1.4 g TF   (0.1
g SAT)   3 g CARB   4 mg S   0 mg CH

The easiest way to chop the hazelnuts is by pulsing them in a food processor fitted with the metal chopping blade.

Preheat the oven to moderately slow (325° F.). Combine ½ cup of the sugar, the egg substitute, and the vanilla in a large bowl and set aside. Toss the hazelnuts with the cornstarch and set aside also. Beat the egg whites until frothy, then add the remaining sugar, 1 tablespoon at a time; continue beating until the meringue is stiff and glossy. Mix about 1 cup of the meringue into the egg substitute mixture, then fold in the balance. Finally, gently but thoroughly fold in the hazelnuts and any loose cornstarch.

Drop from a teaspoon onto baking sheets lightly sprayed with nonstick vegetable cooking spray, spacing the meringues about 2 inches apart. Bake 20 to 25 minutes in the preheated oven until lightly browned. Cool on the baking sheets until crisp—1 to 2 minutes—then transfer to wire racks to cool completely. Store airtight.

ORANGE MACAROONS

MAKES ABOUT 4 DOZEN

½ cup granulated sugar
½ cup unsifted confectioners' sugar
1½ (7.5-ounce) packages almond paste,
cut into small dice
1 tablespoon finely grated orange zest
1 teaspoon Grand Marnier
½ teaspoon vanilla
2 extra-large egg whites

PER COOKIE: 44C 1 g P 1.8 g TF (0.2
g SAT) 6 g CARB 3 mg S 0 mg CH

Simply wonderful—and totally devoid of cholesterol and almost all saturated fats! Note: If you have a food processor, you'll find these macaroons a snap to make. Equip it with the metal chopping blade and churn the 2 sugars, the almond paste, orange zest, Grand Marnier, and vanilla for 1 to 1½ minutes until smooth, then pulse in the egg whites, one by one. That's all there is to it.

Preheat the oven to moderately slow (325° F.). Line 3 baking sheets with baking parchment and set aside. Mix the granulated and confectioners' sugars, the almond paste, orange zest, Grand Marnier, and vanilla until smooth. Beat in the egg whites, one at a time.

Drop from a teaspoon onto the prepared baking sheets, spacing the macaroons about 2 inches apart. Bake 18 to 20 minutes in the preheated oven until pale tan. Cool the macaroons on the parchment on the baking sheets. To remove, set the parchment on a kitchen towel dipped in cold water and wrung out—not too dry—and let stand 1 to 2 minutes. Carefully peel off the meringues and set them on a wire rack. Let air-dry several hours, then store airtight.

5

*I*CES,

SHERBETS,

AND

OTHER

FROZEN

DESSERTS

FROZEN FUDGE MOUSSE

MAKES 8 SERVINGS

3½ teaspoons unflavored gelatin

½ cup superfine sugar

⅓ cup unsweetened Dutch process cocoa powder

2 teaspoons instant espresso coffee crystals

2 cups evaporated skim milk, at room temperature

1 tablespoon unsalted soft tub margarine (not extra-light)

1 ounce semisweet chocolate, coarsely chopped (optional)

1½ teaspoons vanilla

¼ cup boiling water

3 tablespoons meringue powder (see page xviii)

1½ cups partially frozen evaporated skim milk (a 12-ounce can)

1 teaspoon freshly squeezed lemon juice

PER SERVING: 175 C   11 g P   2.3 g TF   (0.7 g SAT)   29 g CARB   165 mg S   4.5 mg CH

So smooth it's hard to believe it contains no egg yolks or cream. For a richer mousse, add the optional ounce of semisweet chocolate. It will increase the amount of saturated fat, it's true. But only slightly *since that ounce is spread over 8 servings.* Note: If evaporated skim milk is to whip impressively, you must partially freeze it and have the beaters and bowl ice cold, too. I usually set an unopened can of milk in the freezer for 2½ to 3 hours and put the beaters and bowl into the freezer for the last half hour.

Combine the gelatin, 2 tablespoons of the sugar, the cocoa, and coffee crystals in a medium-size heavy saucepan; stir in the room-temperature milk and let stand 5 minutes. Set over moderately low heat and cook and stir 3 to 5 minutes until the gelatin dissolves completely. Add the margarine and, if you like, the chocolate, and cook and stir about 3 minutes until smooth. Pour into a large heatproof bowl and mix in the vanilla. Set in an ice bath and chill, stirring often, for 20 to 25 minutes or until the mixture mounds nicely when you take a little bit of it up on a spoon. Set aside.

In a medium-size heatproof bowl, combine the remaining sugar and the boiling water. Add the meringue powder and beat with a hand mixer at highest speed for 3 to 4 minutes until as stiff and glossy as 7-minute icing. Stir about ½ cup of the meringue into the chocolate mixture, then gently fold in the remainder until there are no streaks of white or brown; set aside.

Empty the partially frozen can of milk into an ice-cold medium-size bowl, add the lemon juice, and beat at highest hand mixer speed for 3 to 4 minutes until thick and billowing—it will not peak stiffly. Fold into the chocolate mixture, pour into a 9 × 5 × 3-inch pan, and freeze 1½ to 2 hours until mushy. Scoop into a large bowl and beat at highest mixer speed until fluffy-light. Return to the pan and to the freezer and freeze about 1 hour until soft-firm. Spoon into dessert goblets and serve. *Note: If the mousse should freeze too hard, soften at room temperature about 30 minutes before serving.*

FROZEN CAFÉ AU LAIT MOUSSE

MAKES 6 SERVINGS

½ cup sugar

¼ cup water

1 tablespoon instant espresso coffee crystals

½ teaspoon ground cinnamon

2 egg whites

Pinch of salt

Pinch of cream of tartar

1½ cups (½ recipe) Mock Whipped Cream (page 174)

OPTIONAL GARNISH:

2 tablespoons crushed Amaretti cookies

PER SERVING: 88 C 2 g P 0 g TF (0 g SAT) 20 g CARB 56 mg S 0.5 mg CH

If this creamy fat-free dessert is to have the proper coffee flavor, you must use the best instant espresso coffee you can find.

Combine the sugar, water, espresso crystals, and cinnamon in a small heavy saucepan, set, uncovered, over moderate heat, and swirl the pan until sugar dissolves. Insert a candy thermometer and cook without stirring until the mixture reaches the soft-ball stage (238° F.). Remove from the heat.

Beat the egg whites until foamy in the small bowl of an electric mixer set at medium speed, add the salt and cream of tartar and beat to stiff peaks. With the motor still running, carefully pour the hot syrup down the side of the bowl into the beaten whites so that it doesn't hit the beaters and spatter all over. Continue beating at medium speed until thick, fluffy, and cool.

Remove the bowl from the mixer, gently fold in the Mock Whipped Cream, and spoon the mousse into 6 (5-ounce) ramekins or parfait glasses. Freeze for at least 4 hours. Sprinkle each portion, if you like, with crushed Amaretti just before serving.

FROZEN APRICOT MOUSSE

MAKES 6 SERVINGS

2 cups freshly squeezed orange juice
6 ounces dried apricots
¾ cup sugar
3 tablespoons water
⅛ teaspoon freshly squeezed lemon juice
2 egg whites
2 cup Mock Whipped Cream (page 174)
3 tablespoons finely chopped crystallized
ginger

PER SERVING: 256 C   4 g P   0.3 g TF
(0 g SAT)   62 g CARB   48 mg S
0.6 mg CH

*B*oil the orange juice gently in an uncovered small, heavy, nonmetallic saucepan over moderate heat about 10 minutes until reduced to 1½ cups. Add the apricots and ¼ cup of the sugar and cook, uncovered, for 5 to 7 minutes until the apricots soften. Remove from the heat, cover, and steep 20 minutes; then purée by churning in a food processor 1 minute; refrigerate while you proceed.

*C*ombine the remaining ½ cup sugar, the water, and the lemon juice in a small heavy saucepan, set, uncovered, over moderate heat, and swirl until the sugar dissolves. Insert a candy thermometer and cook without stirring until the mixture reaches the soft-ball stage (238° F.). Remove from the heat.

*B*eat the egg whites until stiff in the small bowl of an electric mixer set at medium speed. With the motor still running, carefully pour the hot syrup down the side of the bowl into the beaten whites so that it doesn't hit the beaters and spatter all over. Continue beating at medium speed until thick, fluffy, and cool.

*R*emove the bowl from the mixer, gently fold in the apricot purée, the Mock Whipped Cream, and the chopped ginger. Spoon into a 4-cup mold and freeze about 6 hours until firm.

FROZEN RASPBERRY MOUSSE

MAKES 6 SERVINGS

1 (12-ounce) package frozen dry-pack raspberries, thawed but not drained

2 tablespoons framboise (raspberry liqueur)

½ cup sugar

3 tablespoons water

⅛ teaspoon freshly squeezed lemon juice

2 egg whites

1 cup Mock Whipped Cream (page 174)

PER SERVING: 126 C   3 g P   0.6 g TF
(0 g SAT)   28 g CARB   29 mg S
0.3 mg CH

Top, if you like, with Raspberry Sauce (see Île Flotante, page 44).

Purée the raspberries with their juice and the framboise by churning 1 minute in a food processor; force the purée through a fine sieve and discard the seeds. Refrigerate while you proceed.

Combine the sugar, water, and lemon juice in a small heavy saucepan, set, uncovered, over moderate heat, and swirl until the sugar dissolves. Insert a candy thermometer and cook without stirring until the mixture reaches the soft-ball stage (238° F.). Remove from the heat.

Beat the egg whites until stiff in the small bowl of an electric mixer set at medium speed. With the motor still running, carefully pour the hot syrup down the side of the bowl into the beaten whites so that it doesn't hit the beaters and spatter all over. Continue beating at medium speed until thick, fluffy, and cool.

Remove the bowl from the mixer, gently fold in the raspberry purée and Mock Whipped Cream, spoon into a 4-cup mold, and freeze about 6 hours until firm.

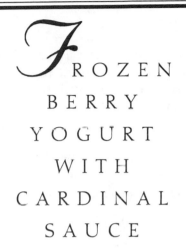

*F*ROZEN BERRY YOGURT WITH CARDINAL SAUCE

MAKES 6 SERVINGS

*1 (10-ounce) package frozen raspberries
in light syrup, partially thawed
but not drained*

*1 (10-ounce) package frozen strawberries
in light syrup, partially thawed
but not drained*

2 cups plain lowfat yogurt

6 tablespoons superfine sugar

1 tablespoon Grand Marnier

¼ teaspoon finely grated orange zest

1 recipe Cardinal Sauce (page 184)

GARNISHES:

*1 cup fresh red raspberries
6 small sprigs fresh mint*

PER SERVING: 294 C   5 g P   1.5 g TF   (0.8
g SAT)   68 g CARB   55 mg S   4.5 mg CH

*P*urée the raspberries and strawberries by churn-ing 1 minute in a food processor. Sieve, if you like, to remove the seeds, then return to the processor. Add the yogurt, sugar, Grand Marnier, and orange zest and churn 20 seconds. Scrape the sides down and churn 30 to 40 seconds longer until smooth. Spoon into a 9 × 9 × 2-inch baking dish and freeze 2 to 2½ hours until soft-firm. Scoop the partially frozen berry yogurt into a food processor and churn 25 to 30 seconds until fluffy. Spoon back into the pan and freeze about 1 hour until soft-firm.

*T*o serve, layer scoops of the berry yogurt and Cardinal Sauce alternately into 6 parfait glasses, ending with a drizzling of sauce. Tuck a few rasp-berries in and around the final scoop of frozen yogurt and garnish each portion with a mint sprig.

FRESH BANANA ICE CREAM

MAKES 8 SERVINGS

¼ cup sugar

1 package unflavored gelatin

½ cup light corn syrup

1½ cups evaporated skim milk

5 medium-size ripe bananas, peeled
(about 1¾ pounds)

1 cup freshly squeezed orange juice

⅓ cup freshly squeezed lemon juice

2 teaspoons finely grated orange zest

½ teaspoon vanilla

OPTIONAL GARNISH:

8 twists of orange or lemon

PER SERVING: 201 C   5 g P   0.5 g TF   (0.2
g SAT)   46 g CARB   87 mg S   1.9 mg CH

This contains no cream of any kind, and yet it's smooth and rich.

Combine the sugar and gelatin in a small heavy saucepan, mix in the corn syrup and milk, set over moderately low heat, and cook and stir 5 to 7 minutes until the gelatin dissolves completely; don't let the mixture boil or the milk may curdle. Purée the bananas with the orange and lemon juices, the orange zest, and the vanilla by churning in a food processor 1 minute; add the gelatin mixture and pulse 10 to 12 times to incorporate.

Pour into a 9 × 5 × 3-inch loaf pan and freeze 2 hours until mushy. Scoop the partially frozen ice cream into the food processor and churn 25 to 30 seconds until fluffy. Spoon back into the loaf pan and freeze about 1 hour until soft-firm. Mound the ice cream into goblets and garnish each serving, if you like, with a twist of orange or lemon.

HONEY-PINE NUT ICE CREAM

MAKES 8 SERVINGS

½ cup golden seedless raisins (sultanas)

⅓ cup amaretto, Frangelico, Marsala, or light rum

3 tablespoons water

½ cup pine nuts or slivered blanched almonds

1 pound lowfat (1 percent) cottage cheese or ricotta

½ cup honey

⅓ cup miniature chocolate chips (optional)

PER SERVING: 206 C   10 g P   5.2 g TF
(1.1 g SAT)   30 g CARB
233 mg S   2.3 mg CH

A Sicilian classic stripped of most of its cholesterol and about half its calories.

Steep the raisins in the amaretto and water for 30 minutes. Meanwhile, line an 8 × 4 × 2¾-inch loaf pan with plastic food wrap, leaving a 2-inch overhang all around. Place the pine nuts in a small skillet, set over moderate heat, and toast, tossing frequently, about 4 minutes until golden; set aside.

Purée the cottage cheese by buzzing in a food processor 60 seconds. Add the honey and pulse to combine. Transfer to a medium-size bowl, fold in the raisins and their steeping liquid, the nuts, and, if you like, the chocolate chips. Spoon into the prepared loaf pan, fold the plastic wrap overhang in to cover the cheese mixture, and freeze at least 4 hours until firm.

Lift the loaf from the pan, unwrap, and invert it onto a small platter. Dip a sharp knife into hot water and cut the loaf into slices about ⅜ inch thick. Divide the slices among 8 dessert plates and let soften 5 minutes before serving.

$\mathcal{T}$UTTI-FRUTTI PARFAIT WITH TOASTED HAZELNUTS

MAKES 12 SERVINGS

½ cup cold water

2 envelopes unflavored gelatin

2 cups lowfat (1 percent) cottage cheese

2 cups plain lowfat yogurt

1 cup unsifted confectioners' sugar

2 tablespoons Grand Marnier

1 teaspoon vanilla

½ teaspoon almond extract

1 cup moderately finely chopped mixed
candied fruits

½ cup moderately finely chopped
skinned, toasted hazelnuts

PER SERVING: 199 C   8 g P   4 g TF
(0.8 g SAT)   32 g CARB   243 mg S
3.8 mg CH

$\mathcal{F}$or directions on how to toast and skin hazelnuts, see the headnote for Chocolate-Hazelnut Dacquoise (page 92).

$\mathcal{P}$lace the water in a very small, heavy saucepan, sprinkle the gelatin evenly over the surface, and let stand 5 minutes. Set over moderately low heat and cook and stir 3 to 5 minutes until the gelatin dissolves completely. Churn the cottage cheese, yogurt, confectioners' sugar, Grand Marnier, vanilla, and almond extract in a food processor 1 to 1½ minutes until absolutely smooth. Add the hot gelatin in a fine stream, pulsing all the while. By hand, fold in the candied fruits and hazelnuts. Pour into a 9 × 5 × 3-inch loaf pan and freeze about 4 hours until firm. When ready to serve, let the parfait stand at room temperature 30 minutes, then dip quickly into hot water, and unmold on a small platter. Slice ¾ inch thick.

GINGERY PINEAPPLE SHERBET

MAKES 8 SERVINGS

3 cups canned crushed pineapple (3 cans, 8¼ ounces each), with its liquid

1 envelope unflavored gelatin

2 tablespoons very finely minced fresh ginger

½ cup corn syrup

3 cups lowfat buttermilk

½ teaspoon vanilla

¼ teaspoon almond extract

PER SERVING: 154 C   4 g P   0.9 g TF   (0.5 g SAT)   33 g CARB   128 mg S   3.7 mg CH

ow in calories, low in cholesterol, and quick and easy, too. You can, if you like, substitute fresh pineapple for the canned (you'll need a medium-size, dead-ripe pineapple). But if you do, you'll have to increase the amount of corn syrup somewhat. As for crushing the pineapple, you need only peel it, wedge it, core it, and chunk it. The food processor will do the rest.

*M*ix the pineapple, gelatin, ginger, and corn syrup in a small heavy saucepan, set over moderate heat, and cook and stir 5 minutes until the gelatin dissolves completely. Dump into a food processor and churn 10 to 15 seconds until almost smooth. Add the buttermilk, vanilla, and almond extract and pulse 10 to 12 times to incorporate.

*P*our into a 9 × 5 × 3-inch loaf pan and freeze 2 hours until mushy. Scoop the partially frozen sherbet into the food processor and churn 25 to 30 seconds until fluffy. Spoon back into the loaf pan and freeze about 1 hour until soft-firm. Mound the sherbet into goblets and serve.

TROPICAL ISLAND SHERBET

MAKES 4 SERVINGS

*3 medium-size ripe bananas, peeled
(about 1¼ pounds)*

½ cup plain lowfat yogurt

⅓ cup firmly packed dark brown sugar

2 tablespoons dark rum

2 tablespoons freshly squeezed lime juice

⅛ teaspoon freshly grated nutmeg

*½ cup coarsely chopped toasted blanched
almonds*

PER SERVING: 284 C   6 g P   9.4 g TF   (1.3
g SAT)   45 g CARB   28 mg S   1.7 mg CH

ananas make this rich and creamy.

*P*urée the bananas with the yogurt, brown sugar, rum, lime juice, and nutmeg by churning about 1 minute in a food processor. Spoon into an 8 × 8 × 2-inch pan, cover with plastic food wrap, and freeze 2 to 3 hours until firm around the edges and almost firm in the middle. Churn 10 seconds in a food processor until fluffy, return to the pan, fold in the almonds, and freeze until firm.

Tipsy Parson (page 58)

CLOCKWISE FROM TOP RIGHT:
Raisin Cake with Almond Icing (page 124),
Apple Upside-down Cake (page 112),
Angel Roll with Tart Lemon Filling (page 100),
Blond Ginger-bread with Fresh Blueberries (page 119),
Buttermilk Cupcakes with Brown Sugar Frosting (page 137),
Black Forest Cake (page 128)

Riz à L'Impératrice (page 54)

$\mathcal{F}$RESH MANGO- LIME SHERBET

MAKES 8 SERVINGS

⚖

½ cup sugar

1 envelope unflavored gelatin

⅓ cup light corn syrup

½ cup water

*4 large dead-ripe mangoes (4 pounds),
peeled and pitted*

½ teaspoon finely grated lime zest

⅓ cup freshly squeezed lime juice

1 cup lowfat buttermilk

OPTIONAL GARNISH:

8 twists of lime

PER SERVING: 207 C   3 g P   0.7 g TF   (0.3 g SAT)   51 g CARB   56 mg S   1.2 mg CH

$\mathcal{M}$angoes are neither neat nor easy to pit and peel. Even in squishy-ripe fruits, the flesh clings to both the big furry seed and the skin. About the best you can do is scrape the flesh from them with a sharp paring knife. It's tedious work, but this smooth, low-cholesterol sherbet is definitely worth the trouble. Note: Be sure that the lime juice you use is freshly squeezed.

$\mathcal{C}$ombine the sugar and gelatin in a small heavy saucepan, mix in the corn syrup and water, set over moderate heat, and cook and stir about 5 minutes until the gelatin dissolves completely. Purée the mangoes with the lime zest and juice by churning in a food processor 1 minute; add the gelatin mixture and pulse 6 to 8 times to incorporate. Add the buttermilk and churn 10 to 15 seconds until absolutely smooth.

$\mathcal{P}$our into a 9 × 5 × 3-inch loaf pan and freeze 2 hours until mushy. Scoop the partially frozen sherbet into the food processor and churn 25 to 30 seconds until fluffy. Spoon back into the loaf pan and freeze ¾ to 1 hour until soft-firm. Mound the sherbet into goblets and garnish each serving, if you like, with a twist of lime.

V A R I A T I O N :

⚖ $\mathcal{F}$resh $\mathcal{P}$apaya $\mathcal{S}$herbet *(8 servings):* Prepare as directed, substituting 4 pounds of ripe papayas for the mangoes.

PER SERVING: 165 C   3 g P   0.5 g TF   (0.2 g SAT)   40 g CARB   57 mg S   0.2 mg CH

GINGERY CITRUS GRANITA

MAKES 8 SERVINGS

½ cup sugar
1 envelope unflavored gelatin
1 teaspoon finely grated grapefruit zest
1 teaspoon finely grated orange zest
1 teaspoon finely grated lemon zest
1 cup water
2 cups freshly squeezed pink grapefruit
juice
1 cup freshly squeezed orange juice
¼ cup freshly squeezed lemon juice
2 teaspoons fresh ginger juice
½ cup light corn syrup

PER SERVING: 202 C   2 g P   0.2 g TF   (0
g SAT)   50 g CARB   42 mg S   0 mg CH

The easiest way to obtain fresh ginger juice is to press small peeled cubes of fresh ginger through a pristine garlic press.

Combine the sugar, gelatin, citrus zests, and water in a small heavy saucepan. Set over moderate heat and cook and stir about 5 minutes until the gelatin dissolves completely. Remove from the heat and combine with all remaining ingredients. Pour into a 13 × 9 × 2-inch baking pan and freeze 1½ to 2 hours until mushy-firm. Scoop the partially frozen granita into a food processor and churn 25 to 30 seconds until fluffy. Spoon back into the pan and once again freeze until mushy-firm (about 1 hour this time), then churn as before until light and fluffy. Spoon the granita into 2 (1-quart) freezer containers, cover, and store in the freezer. Let the granita stand at room temperature 15 to 20 minutes before serving.

STRAWBERRY SORBET WITH FRESH STRAWBERRY COULIS

MAKES 6 SERVINGS

½ cup cold water

2 envelopes unflavored gelatin

1 quart dead-ripe strawberries, hulled, puréed, and sieved

½ cup superfine sugar

1 cup cranberry juice cocktail

¼ cup light corn syrup

2 tablespoons freshly squeezed lemon juice

1½ teaspoons finely grated orange zest

1 recipe Fresh Strawberry Coulis (page 185)

OPTIONAL GARNISHES:

6 perfect strawberries and/or 2 tablespoons finely shredded orange zest

12 small sprigs lemon verbena, lemon geranium, or mint

PER SERVING: 261 C   3 g P   0.6 g TF   (0 g SAT)   63 g CARB   26 mg S   0 mg CH

This recipe is an adaptation of an extraordinary sorbet I tasted last year at a cozy little restaurant in Quimper, Brittany, called Le Capucin Gourmand. It was made with the intensely flavored Breton strawberries of Plougastel, which are in season right up until October. If you are to approximate their heady bouquet, you must choose sun-ripened berries at their peak of flavor. The hard, tasteless specimens sold year-round at supermarkets just won't do.

*P*lace the water in a very small, heavy saucepan, sprinkle the gelatin evenly over the surface, and let stand 5 minutes. Set over moderately low heat and cook and stir 3 to 5 minutes until the gelatin dissolves completely; remove from the heat and set aside.

*I*n a large, nonmetallic mixing bowl, combine the strawberry purée and the sugar and let stand 20 minutes at room temperature. Stir in the cranberry juice cocktail, corn syrup, lemon juice, and orange zest, then stir in the reserved gelatin. Pour into a 9 × 5 × 3-inch loaf pan and freeze 2 to 2½ hours until mushy. Scoop the partially frozen sorbet into a food processor and churn 25 to 30 seconds until fluffy. Spoon back into the loaf pan and freeze 1 to 1½ hours until firm but not brick-hard.

*T*o serve, puddle about ¼ cup of the Fresh Strawberry Coulis in the well of each of 6 dessert plates, arrange 3 small scoops of sorbet in a triangle in the coulis on each plate, then, if desired, garnish each portion with a perfect strawberry and 2 sprigs of lemon verbena.

CHAPTER

6

SAUCES, CREAMS, AND OTHER TOPPINGS

Mock
WHIPPED CREAM

MAKES 3 CUPS

¾ teaspoon unflavored gelatin
1 tablespoon cold water
½ cup nonfat dry milk powder
½ cup ice water
2 tablespoons confectioners' sugar
1 teaspoon vanilla

PER TABLESPOON: 4 C   LESS THAN 1 g P
0 g TF (0 g SAT)   1 g CARB   4 mg S
0.1 mg CH

A fluffy, all-purpose topping that can double as a filling. Properly whipped, it will be stiff enough to mound or to pipe through a pastry bag.

Soften the gelatin in the cold water in a small heatproof measuring cup. Set the cup in a pan of simmering water and heat about 4 minutes until the gelatin dissolves; remove from the heat. Combine the dry milk, ice water, and confectioners' sugar in the chilled small bowl of an electric mixer, then beat with chilled beaters at medium speed until foamy. With the motor running, carefully pour the gelatin down the side of the bowl so that it doesn't hit the beaters and spatter all over. Continue beating at medium speed for 7 to 10 minutes until it is the texture of whipped cream, then beat in the vanilla. If not using immediately, store in the refrigerator. If the mixture should deflate on standing, simply beat until it again resembles whipped cream.

CRÈME FRAÎCHE

MAKES ABOUT 1¼ CUPS

1 cup plain lowfat yogurt
¼ cup lowfat buttermilk
½ teaspoon sugar

PER TABLESPOON: 9 C   1 g P   0.2 g TF (0.1 g SAT)   1 g CARB   11 mg S   0.8 mg CH

Wonderful ladled over any fresh berries or sliced ripe peaches or nectarines.

Combine the yogurt, buttermilk, and sugar in a small bowl. Let stand at room temperature for 6 hours, then refrigerate for several hours before serving.

$\mathcal{L}$ABNA

MAKES ABOUT 1¾ CUPS

1 quart nonfat yogurt, drained well

<u>PER TABLESPOON</u>: 11 C   1 g P   0 g TF
(0 g SAT)   1 g CARB   11 mg S   0 mg CH

This Middle Eastern staple is nothing more than plain nonfat yogurt that has been set to drain in the refrigerator for about a day. Once all the sour whey has run off, you're left with a thick, mild, creamy curd. Whisk it hard and it's smooth as silk. You can use it in recipes in place of sour cream or plain yogurt; you can ladle it over fresh fruits, pies, cobblers, and crisps. In India it's sometimes sweetened and scented with rose water or orange flower water, but it's every bit as good flavored with vanilla, or with finely grated lemon or orange zest.

$\mathcal{L}$ine a large fine sieve with 4 thicknesses of cheesecloth, set the sieve over a large bowl, then dump in the yogurt. Cut through the yogurt criss-cross fashion with a knife, bring the ends of the cheesecloth up over the yogurt so that it is completely covered, then let stand undisturbed in the refrigerator for about 24 hours. Discard all liquid that has drained off—there will be plenty—then spoon the Labna into a 1-pint jar, cover, and store in the refrigerator.

V A R I A T I O N S :

✤ *East Indian Labna (1¾ cups):* Prepare the Labna as directed, then whisk in 2 tablespoons superfine sugar and 1 teaspoon rose water or orange flower water.

PER TABLESPOON: 15 C   1 g P   0 g TF (0 g SAT)   2 g CARB   11 mg S   0 mg CH

✤ *Vanilla Labna (1¾ cups):* Prepare the Labna as directed, then whisk in 2 tablespoons superfine sugar and ½ teaspoon vanilla.

PER TABLESPOON: 15 C   1 g P   0 g TF (0 g SAT)   2 g CARB   11 mg S   0 mg CH

✤ *Orange or Lemon Labna (1¾ cups):* Prepare the Labna as directed, then whisk in 2 tablespoons superfine sugar and 1 teaspoon finely grated orange or lemon zest.

PER TABLESPOON: 15 C   1 g P   0 g TF (0 g SAT)   2 g CARB   11 mg S   0 mg CH

CRÈME ANGLAISE (CUSTARD SAUCE)

MAKES 2⅓ CUPS

1¾ cups whole milk
¼ cup evaporated skim milk
⅓ cup sugar
1½ teaspoons unsalted soft tub margarine (not extra-light)
1 vanilla bean, split lengthwise
½ cup liquid egg substitute

PER TABLESPOON: 18 C   1 g P   0.5 g TF
(0.3 g SAT)   3 g CARB   12 mg S
1.7 mg CH

The perfect topper for poached fruits, angel food cake, soufflés, and mousses.

Bring the whole milk, evaporated milk, sugar, margarine, and vanilla bean to a simmer in a small heavy saucepan over moderate heat. Beat a little of the hot milk mixture into the egg substitute, stir back into the pan, and cook and stir over moderately low heat until the custard thickens enough to coat a metal spoon. This may take as long as 20 minutes, so have patience. If you try to hurry things along by raising the heat, you risk curdling the custard. As soon as the sauce has thickened, remove from the heat and strain it through a fine sieve. Scrape the tiny black seeds inside the vanilla bean into the custard and mix well; discard the bean. Serve the sauce hot or cold.

VARIATIONS:

Tipsy Custard Sauce (2⅓ cups): Prepare the Crème Anglaise as directed, then, after sieving, stir in 1 tablespoon bourbon or Irish whiskey.

PER TABLESPOON: 19 C   1 g P   0.5 g TF (0.3 g SAT)   3 g CARB   12 mg S
1.7 mg CH

Butterscotch Custard Sauce (2⅓ cups): Prepare the Crème Anglaise as directed, but substitute ⅓ cup firmly packed light brown sugar for the granulated sugar.

PER TABLESPOON: 19 C   1 g P   0.5 g TF (0.3 g SAT)   3 g CARB   13 mg S
1.7 mg CH

Orange Custard Sauce (2⅓ cups): Prepare the Crème Anglaise as directed, but omit the vanilla bean. After straining the sauce, stir in 2 teaspoons Grand Marnier and ½ teaspoon very finely grated orange zest.

PER TABLESPOON: 19 C   1 g P   0.5 g TF (0.3 g SAT)   3 g CARB   12 mg S
1.7 mg CH

✤ *Lemon Custard Sauce (2⅓ cups):* Prepare the Crème Anglaise as directed, but omit the vanilla bean. After straining the sauce, stir in 1 teaspoon lemon extract and ½ teaspoon very finely grated lemon zest.

PER TABLESPOON: 19 C   1 g P   0.5 g TF (0.3 g SAT)   3 g CARB   12 mg S   1.7 mg CH

✤ *Chocolate Custard Sauce (2⅓ cups):* Prepare the Crème Anglaise as directed, but at the outset, blend 2 tablespoons unsweetened Dutch process cocoa powder with the sugar and bring to a simmer along with the milk, evaporated skim milk, and margarine. Omit the vanilla bean and stir 1 teaspoon vanilla into the finished sauce.

PER TABLESPOON: 19 C   1 g P   0.6 g TF (0.3 g SAT)   3 g CARB   14 mg S   1.7 mg CH

✤ *Mocha Custard Sauce (2⅓ cups):* Prepare the Chocolate Custard Sauce as directed, but reduce the cocoa to 1 tablespoon, add 2 teaspoons instant espresso coffee crystals, combine both with the sugar, and bring to a simmer along with the milk, evaporated milk, and margarine.

PER TABLESPOON: 17 C   1 g P   0.5 g TF (0.3 g SAT)   3 g CARB   12 mg S   1.6 mg CH

PASTRY CREAM

MAKES 2 CUPS

2 cups whole milk
⅔ cup sugar
Pinch of salt
6 egg whites
2 tablespoons cornstarch
1 teaspoon vanilla
1 tablespoon unsalted soft tub margarine
(not extra-light)

PER TABLESPOON: 34 C   1 g P   0.8 g TF
(0.4 g SAT)   5 g CARB   22 mg S
2.1 mg CH

You'll hardly believe that this rich cake and pastry filling contains no egg yolks or cream. For an even lower-cholesterol, lower-calorie version, use lowfat (1 or 2 percent) milk instead of whole milk.

Combine the milk, ⅓ cup of the sugar, and the salt in a medium-size heavy saucepan; set, uncovered, over moderate heat and warm just until small bubbles appear around the edge of the pan. Whisk the egg whites with the remaining ⅓ cup sugar and blend in the cornstarch. Whisk a little of the hot mixture into the egg white mixture, then stir back into the pan. Cook, stirring constantly, over moderate heat about 3 minutes until the mixture thickens and no raw starch taste remains. Strain into a medium-size heatproof bowl, then stir in the vanilla and margarine. Place a sheet of wax paper flat on the surface of the cream to prevent a "skin" from forming, cool to room temperature, and refrigerate until ready to use.

$\mathcal{H}$OT

FUDGE

SAUCE

MAKES 2½ CUPS

4 tablespoons all-purpose flour

1 tablespoon cornstarch

¼ cup unsweetened Dutch process cocoa powder

½ cup superfine sugar

1 teaspoon instant espresso coffee crystals (optional)

2 cups evaporated skim milk

2 tablespoons unsalted soft tub margarine (not extra-light)

1 teaspoon vanilla

PER TABLESPOON: 30 C   1 g P   0.7 g TF (0.2 g SAT)   5 g CARB   19 mg S 0.5 mg CH

$\mathcal{U}$nbelievably smooth, unbelievably rich, and yet very low in saturated fat and cholesterol. This pared-down Hot Fudge Sauce also contains less than half the calories of "the real thing." You needn't add the espresso coffee crystals, but they do deepen and mellow the flavor of the cocoa.

$\mathcal{B}$lend the flour, cornstarch, cocoa, sugar, and coffee crystals in a small heavy saucepan, pressing out all lumps. Mix in the milk, set over moderate heat, and cook, stirring constantly, about 3 minutes until thickened and smooth. Add the margarine, reduce the heat to moderately low, and cook and stir 2 to 3 minutes until the margarine has melted and the sauce is satin-smooth. Remove from the heat and stir in the vanilla. Serve hot or warm, over ice milk, frozen yogurt, or—to be really decadent—over Frozen Fudge Mousse (page 158).

BUTTER-SCOTCH SAUCE

MAKES 2 CUPS

2 tablespoons extra-light olive oil or
vegetable oil (canola, safflower, sunflower, corn oil, etc.)

1 tablespoon cornstarch

½ cup firmly packed dark brown sugar

2 tablespoons dark corn syrup

1½ cups evaporated skim milk

1 tablespoon freshly squeezed lemon
juice

1½ teaspoons vanilla

½ teaspoon butter flavor granules

PER TABLESPOON: 35 C   1 g P   0.9 g TF
(0.1 g SAT)   6 g CARB   20 mg S
0.5 mg CH

Delicious over Cloud-High Angel Food Cake (page 102), sliced fresh peaches or oranges, ice milk, or frozen yogurt.

Blend the oil and cornstarch in a medium-size heavy saucepan and cook and stir over moderate heat for 1 minute. Mix in the sugar, corn syrup, and milk and cook, stirring constantly, about 3 minutes until the mixture bubbles up, thickens, and clears. Remove from the heat and stir in the lemon juice, vanilla, and butter granules. Serve hot, warm, or at room temperature.

CARAMEL SAUCE

MAKES ABOUT ¾ CUP

½ cup sugar
⅓ cup water
1 teaspoon freshly squeezed lemon juice
½ cup evaporated skim milk
1½ teaspoons unsalted soft tub
    margarine (not extra-light)
1 teaspoon vanilla

PER TABLESPOON: 46 C   1 g P   0.4 g TF
    (0.1 g SAT)   10 g CARB   12 mg S
        0.4 mg CH

Serve with poached pears or peaches, or ladle over any plain low-fat, low-cholesterol cake or ice milk.

Combine the sugar, water, and lemon juice in a small heavy saucepan, set over moderate heat, and cook and stir until the sugar has dissolved. Stop stirring but continue cooking, uncovered, until the mixture is amber in color—about 5 minutes. Add the milk and margarine without stirring, bring to a boil, and boil, uncovered, 1 minute. Remove from the heat and stir in the vanilla. Serve warm or at room temperature.

CARDINAL SAUCE

MAKES ABOUT 1½ CUPS

1 (10-ounce) package frozen raspberries in light syrup, thawed but not drained

¼ cup low-sugar strawberry jam

1 tablespoon superfine sugar

1½ teaspoons cornstarch

PER TABLESPOON: 22 C 0 g P 0 g TF
(0 g SAT) 6 g CARB 0 mg S 0 mg CH

*D*rain the raspberries in a large strainer set over a bowl; reserve the juices and set aside. Dump the raspberries into a food processor, add the jam, and churn 20 seconds until smooth. Strain through a fine sieve and set the purée aside. Measure the reserved raspberry juice, and, if necessary, add cold water to measure ½ cup.

*C*ombine the sugar and cornstarch in a small, heavy saucepan, add the raspberry juice, set over low heat, and cook, stirring constantly, until the mixture bubbles up and turns clear, about 3 minutes. Remove from the heat and blend into the raspberry purée. Cover and refrigerate until ready to serve.

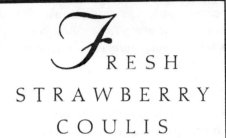

$\mathcal{F}$RESH STRAWBERRY COULIS

MAKES 2 CUPS

1 pint dead-ripe strawberries, hulled,
puréed, and sieved

¼ cup superfine sugar

1½ teaspoons finely grated orange zest

1 teaspoon freshly squeezed lemon juice

1 tablespoon Grand Marnier

¼ cup melted and sieved red raspberry
preserves

PER TABLESPOON: 17 C   0 g P   0 g TF
(0 g SAT)   4 g CARB   0 mg S   0 mg CH

$\mathcal{S}$uperb with fruit sorbets, or ladled over fresh summer fruits or angel food cake.

Combine the strawberry purée, sugar, orange zest, lemon juice, and Grand Marnier in a medium-size, nonmetallic bowl and let stand 20 minutes at room temperature. Blend in the raspberry preserves, cover, and chill until ready to serve.

ORANGE SAUCE

MAKES ABOUT 1½ CUPS

1 tablespoon extra-light olive oil or
vegetable oil (canola, safflower, sunflower, corn oil, etc.)

1 tablespoon cornstarch

⅔ cup sugar

1 tablespoon finely grated orange zest

½ cup freshly squeezed orange juice

3 tablespoons freshly squeezed lemon
juice

¼ cup liquid egg substitute

PER TABLESPOON: 31 C   0 g P   1 g TF (0.1
g SAT)   7 g CARB   3 mg S   0 mg CH

Try ladling this tart sauce over Orange Soufflé (page 48), Citrus Cake (page 117), Fresh Ginger Cake with Orange (page 118), or almost any yellow or white cake. Store any leftover sauce in the refrigerator. Warm slowly in the top of a double boiler before serving, thinning, if necessary, with 1 to 2 tablespoons of hot water.

Blend the oil with the cornstarch, sugar, and orange zest in a medium-size heavy saucepan, then mix in the orange and lemon juices. Cook and stir over moderate heat about 3 minutes until the mixture boils, thickens, and clears. Remove from the heat. Place the egg substitute in a medium-size heatproof bowl, then *very slowly* pour in the hot orange mixture, whisking hard all the while. *Note: Take care that you don't add the orange mixture too fast because the egg substitute may curdle. If it should, despite all precautions, simply put the finished sauce through a fine sieve.* Serve hot, warm, or at room temperature.

FARO APRICOT SAUCE

MAKES ABOUT 2½ CUPS

2 (1-pound) cans peeled apricot halves, with their liquid

2 tablespoons freshly squeezed lemon juice

1 tablespoon finely grated orange zest

1 teaspoon finely grated lemon zest

⅔ cup firmly packed light brown sugar

¼ cup superfine sugar

1 cinnamon stick, broken in half

1 tablespoon unsalted soft tub margarine (not extra-light)

PER TABLESPOON: 34 C 0 g P 0.3 g TF (0.1 g SAT) 8 g CARB 2 mg S 0 mg CH

A superb topping for Algarve Poached Meringue Ring (page 45), Cloud-High Angel Food Cake (page 102), sliced ripe peaches or navel oranges.

Churn the apricots and their liquid in a food processor 1 to 1½ minutes until absolutely smooth. Add the lemon juice, orange and lemon zests, and the brown and superfine sugars and pulse 8 to 10 times to mix. Empty into a large heavy saucepan, drop in the cinnamon stick, set over moderate heat, and bring to a boil. Reduce the heat so that the mixture bubbles *very gently*, and simmer, uncovered, ¾ to 1 hour until thick and the color of caramel. *Note: You'll have to stir often, especially toward the end of cooking, to keep the sauce from scorching.* Remove from the heat, discard the cinnamon stick, add the margarine, and stir until melted. Serve warm or at room temperature.

Nutmeg Sauce

MAKES ABOUT 1¼ CUPS

¾ cup sugar
2 tablespoons all-purpose flour
¾ teaspoon freshly grated nutmeg
1 cup water
1 tablespoon cider vinegar
½ teaspoon freshly squeezed lemon juice

PER TABLESPOON: 32 C   0 g P   0 g TF
(0 g SAT)   10 g CARB   0 mg S   0 mg CH

Delicious ladled over fruit cobblers, pound cake, or yellow cake. If the sauce is to have proper nutmeg flavor, it's essential that you grate the nutmeg yourself. Commercially ground nutmeg has a bitter aftertaste and lacks the delicate lemony bouquet of the freshly grated.

Combine the sugar, flour, and nutmeg in a small heavy saucepan, then stir in the water, vinegar, and lemon juice. Set over moderate heat and cook, stirring constantly, until the sauce is thickened and smooth and no raw floury taste remains—about 5 minutes. Serve hot.

$\mathcal{I}$NDEX

Fudge
frozen fudge mousse, 158–59
hot fudge sauce, 181

Ginger
carrot-ginger cake with orange glaze, 122–23
ginger and walnut pie, 76
ginger cake with orange, 118
ginger soufflé, 50–51
gingery citrus granita, 170
gingery pineapple sherbet, 167
soft ginger cookies, 144
Gingerbread with fresh blueberries, 119
Glazed orange tofu cheesecake, 72
Glazes
chocolate, 127
orange, 72, 121, 123
red currant jelly, 109
snowy, 146–47
Graham cracker pie crust, 67
Grand Marnier, spicy pumpkin pie with, 73
Granita, gingery citrus, 170
Grapefruits
gingery citrus granita, 170
grapefruit cake, 116
Grapes
layered summer fruits with orange yogurt sauce, 26–27
Gratin of fresh strawberries, 6–7
Gratin, Scott M., xiv

Hazelnuts, xiii
chocolate-hazelnut dacquoise, 92–94

chocolate hazelnut pudding, steamed, 36–37
hazelnut angel food bundt cake, 106
hazelnut meringues, 154
toasting of, 92
tutti-frutti parfait with toasted hazelnuts, 166
vanillekipferl (German vanilla crescents), 150–51
Honey
honey-pine nut ice cream, 165
honey-yogurt-blueberry crêpes, 18
Hot fudge sauce, 181
Hungarian noodle pudding, 56

Icebox cookies, 145
Ice cream, xiii
banana, 164
honey-pine nut, 165
Icing, almond, 125
Île Flotante, 44

Jellies
port wine jelly, 62
red currant jelly glaze, 109

Kiwi fruit
pavlova, 24–25

Labna, xvii
basic recipe, 176
East Indian, 177
lemon, 177
orange, 177
vanilla, 177
Lacy oatmeal cookies, 142
Laranjas à Lisbonense (Lisbon-style oranges), 30
Lattice-top cherry pie with

ground almond crust, 82
Layered summer fruits with orange yogurt sauce, 26–27
Lebkuchen, 146–47
Lemons
angel roll with tart lemon filling, 100–1
citrus cake, 117
gingery citrus granita, 170
lemon angel pie, 88–89
lemon chess pie, 74
lemon custard sauce, 179
lemon labna, 177
lemon-poppy seed cake, 114–15
lemon syrup, 115
lemon-walnut icebox cookies, 145
Limes
citrus cake, 117
lime angel pie, 89
mango-lime sherbet, 169
Little Linzers, 80–81
Low-cholesterol cheese pie, 68–69
Low-cholesterol desserts, characteristics of, xiii–xv
Low-cholesterol graham cracker crust, 67
Low-cholesterol pie crust, 64–65

Macaroons
date-oatmeal macaroon pie, 78
orange macaroons, 155
Mango-lime sherbet, 169
Marbleized chocolate-almond cheese pie, 70
Margarine, xiii–xiv, xviii

ABOUT THE AUTHOR

Jean Anderson holds a B.S. degree in Food and Nutrition from Cornell University as well as an M.S. in Journalism from Columbia University. She has been a food editor for both newspapers and magazines, is a frequent contributor to Bon Appétit, Family Circle, Food & Wine, Gourmet, *and other national magazines, and is the author of thirteen cookbooks including* The Food of Portugal *and* The New Doubleday Cookbook *(with Elaine Hanna). A four-time winner of the* "Cookbook Oscar," *she lives in New York City.*